The GOD of the MOUNTAIN

BOOK II

Wherefore HE SAITH, When He ascended up on high, he led captivity captive, AND GAVE GIFTS UNTO MEN. ...

And HE GAVE SOME, Apostles; and some, Prophets; and some, Evangelists; and some, Pastors and Teachers;
For the perfecting of the saints,
for the work of the ministry,
for the edifying of the Body of Christ:
Till WE ALL COME IN THE UNITY OF THE FAITH,
and of the knowledge of the Son of God, unto a perfect man,
unto the measure of the stature of the fulness of Christ:

Ephesians 4:8, 11-13 KJV

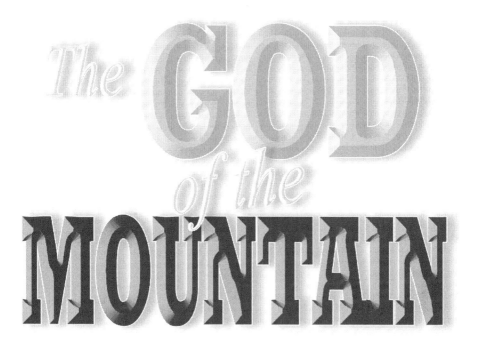

BOOK II

Written by various Authors
(See Contents for a complete list of Authors)

A BOLD TRUTH Publication
Christian Literature & Artwork

The GOD of the MOUNTAIN (BOOK II)
Copyright © 2019 Aaron D. Jones
ISBN 13: 978-1-949993-03-5

First Edition

BOLD TRUTH PUBLISHING
(Christian Literature & Artwork)
606 West 41st, Ste. 4
Sand Springs, Oklahoma 74063
www.BoldTruthPublishing.com

Available from Amazon.com and other retail outlets.
Orders by U.S. trade bookstores and wholesalers.
Email: *boldtruthbooks@yahoo.com*

Quantity sales special discounts are available on quantity purchases by corporations, associations, and others. For details, contact the publisher at the address above.

Artwork, formatting and overall design by Aaron Jones.

Cover photograph used by permission.

Printed in the USA.
03 19   10 9 8 7 6 5 4 3 2 1

Permissions

Scripture quotations marked "AMP" are taken from the Amplified® Bible, Copyright © 1954, 1958, 1962, 1964, 1965, 1987 by The Lockman Foundation. Used by permission.

"Scripture quotations are from the ESV® Bible (The Holy Bible, English Standard Version®), copyright © 2001 by Crossway, a publishing ministry of Good News Publishers. Used by permission. All rights reserved."

Many of the unmarked Scripture quotations and those marked KJV are taken from the King James Version of The Bible. [Public Domain]

"Scripture quotations marked NASB are taken from the New American Standard Bible®, Copyright © 1960, 1962, 1963, 1968, 1971, 1972, 1973, 1975, 1977, 1995 by The Lockman Foundation. Used by permission."

Scriptures marked NKJV are taken from the NEW KING JAMES VERSION (NKJV): Scripture taken from the NEW KING JAMES VERSION®. Copyright© 1982 by Thomas Nelson, Inc. Used by permission. All rights reserved.

"Scripture quotations marked NIV are taken from the Holy Bible, New International Version®. NIV®. Copyright © 1973, 1978, 1984 by International Bible Society. Used by permission of Zondervan. All rights reserved."

"Scripture quotations marked (NLT) are taken from the Holy Bible, New Living Translation, Copyright © 1996,

Permissions

Contents by Author

Contents

Contents

Contents

Contents

Contents

Contents

Foreword

by Wayne Sanders

Therefore encourage one another and build each other up, just as in fact you are doing.
> *- 1 Thessalonians 5:13 NIV*

There is a tremendous wealth of information within the content of this book that I believe will inspire you, teach you, and edify you to receive more knowledge of the love God has in store for you.

This collection of writings has come from numerous authors who have prayerfully selected a moment out of their experiences in ministry, or it may be a devotional, a psalm, a story, or a teaching to give you the reader words that come straight from the heart of God Himself.

A good friend of mine once said this to me, that *"None of us have it all together, but together we have it all."* Although our gifts may differ with each individual, there is a thread that gives us all common ground and that thread is Jesus Christ.

As you read this book I pray and hope you will be inspired by each author, that you will be able to pull on each ministry gift in written form and that you will learn to stand in victory—giving praise to God.

"And they overcame him by the blood of the Lamb and by the word of their testimony, and they did not love their lives to death" - Revelations 12:11 NKJV

Foreword

It never seems to fail that God has a way of making sure that we get the encouragement we need to keep on going at just the right moment. The testimonies we have in our lives serve to not only help us keep going, but also those around us. Just think about how many times you've heard the story of someone else and found strength.

The following writings are inspirations, poems, revelations, songs, teachings and testimonies that we think you will find just as uplifting as we do.

Acknowledgments iii

As a Minister of The Gospel and a Publisher, I would like to thank the following people for helping to bring me to this place in my life and ministry, and for helping make this incredible book possible.

SPECIAL THANKS to (my beautiful wife) Anita Jones; and fellow ministers: George Ballew, Pastor Steve Farmer, Michael Hicks, Daryl Holloman, Jim Isreal, Dr. Rachel Jeffries, Dr. Dave Leggett, Ed Marr, Brian Ohse, Pastors Lionicio & Alma Perez, Dean & Ruth Remmers, Wayne Sanders, Elizabeth Pruitt Sloan, Brad Stine, Pastor Kenn Watson, Kim Wear and (the late Ronnie Moore and Rigoberto Perez) for speaking into my life and ministry— you all share in this ministry's eternal rewards.

Again to Daryl Holloman and Jim Isreal, my Board Members, intercessors, and trusted Friends. Much appreciation and love to both of you, without your examples of faith, fellowship, input, prayers and support, none of this would be possible.

A BIG GOD BLESS YOU and THANK YOU to all the Ministers and Authors that contributed your writings, time, money and prayers into this project. You are all an integral part of God's great mission to the lost and forgotten of this old world. Working together, we are making the GOOD NEWS of God's Son, JESUS CHRIST known in all the Earth.

Acknowledgments

Introduction

I have been a 'paid publisher' for myself and other Christian Authors since January of 2014. God has blessed me in that, as a publisher I get to read everyone's materials (teachings, revelations, testimonies, etc.); and work with some of God's most gifted leadership.

The challenge about leaders is: by their very nature, they are assertive, bold, and strong in their convictions. Someone once said, *"Working with leaders is like trying to herd cats. Every one of them has their own way of doing things."* But I love them, and God has called me and positioned me to work with all of them (the Apostles, Prophets, Evangelists, Pastors and Teachers) as well as those called as: Artists, Authors, Educators, Encouragers, Exhorters, Helps, Poets, and Songwriters.

This Devotional is a testimony to the unifying power of the Holy Ghost of God, [for we are all one Body in Him], and has been brought together, put together and produced under His direction.

In August 2017, Prophet Charles Althouse prophesied to me at a small church just outside of Vinita, Oklahoma:
> *"Aaron Jones, you about to do a project for God. I don't know why He is calling it a project because it has to do with your publishing company. But I'm hearing you are going to do a project. It's going to bless a lot of people ...and it is going to make a lot of money! I mean this thing is going to go, it's going to get big—I'm hearing the word 'viral'...,* then he kinda laughed and said,

"and I don't even know what viral means! But that's what I am hearing, that this thing is going to go viral."

I believe this "GOD of the MOUNTAIN" series of books is that project. Thus far, (the first two volumes) the response has been overwhelming, with over 66 different Authors contributing over 240 different inspired writings, and many requesting how to purchase the books even before their completion.

I think I speak for all of the Authors, when I say, *"It is our prayer that you (the reader) receive this book in the same way that it came together—in the spirit of unity and the bond of peace. Believing it will jump start your day with the Lord and be a blessing to you and your family or ministry.*

"Blessings and much love to you in the all-powerful, unmatched Name of God's only Son—Jesus!"

Sincerely,
Aaron Jones

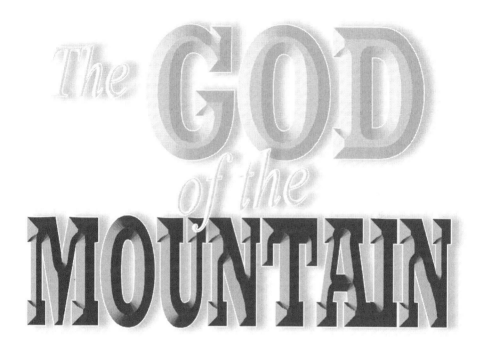

BOOK II

～

DON'T LET YOUR HARVEST REMAIN ON THE VINE
by Barbara J. White

God has established laws in both the natural realm and the spiritual realm. *The law of sowing and reaping,* works just as effectively as the law of gravity. The farmer reaps a harvest from the seeds he has sown in the earth. In the same way, we as believers are destined to reap harvests from the seeds (the Word of God, money, time and things) we have sown into the Kingdom of God.

Weariness can set in, if we don't see our harvest come as soon as we would like. Each seed in the natural realm has its particular growing season – some short and others longer. This is why Paul said in *Galatians 6:9* to *"not lose heart and grow weary and faint ... in due time and the appointed season we shall reap ..."*

Be confident that every seed you have sown, especially in the financial realm, is producing a harvest that is credited to your account. Jesus said that our harvest would come back to us, *"pressed down, shaken together and running over" (Luke 6:38).* Living to give, should be a way of life for every believer. Your harvest is coming in due time! Guaranteed!

The time between sowing and reaping varies. Being consumed with time, can cause discouragement. Exercising faith that your harvest is coming, produces a rest in our soul, and a confident knowing in our spirit, that harvest time is sure to come. God will never fail us.

Don't neglect to claim and receive your harvest of increase. Faith is involved in our sowing, and faith is necessary in obtaining our harvest. The enemy would have us complacent about harvest time. I want to encourage you today, to exercise an aggressive faith in the area of financial harvests. Put God in remembrance of His Word, declare that your harvest is coming - and in many instances is already there waiting to be claimed! Claim what belongs to you, your name is on it. It is credited to your heavenly account *(Phil 4:17)*. Live in joyful expectation as you harvest your financial blessings with your mouth. Your *faith is released* with the words of your mouth! God gives seed to the sower and bread to the eater *(2 Corinthians 9:10)*.

FAITHFUL TO HIS CHILDREN
by Len Blanchard

One of my church members was once faced with a seemingly, difficult decision. He worked for a city water treatment plant. His supervisors asked him to falsify some records on an occasion due to standards not being met for the water. JS was in a tough spot. He was married with four children. He knew that to say no would probably cost him his job. He came to me one evening to share his situation and to get my point of view. JS was a man of honesty, but now it would be tested. It was easy to tell that he was leaning to falsifying the records for this one time. I said, *"Let's pray and ask God what to do."* He said, *"Do you really think He will tell me? I've prayed and prayed with no answer."* Although I was a little fearful I did believe with all my heart God would give an answer.

I asked him to kneel by a small sofa in my office while I kneeled at a large one. As we began to silently pray I said to the Lord, *"If this is going to work You must tell me exactly what you will tell him."* I waited and prayed and waited and prayed. Finally, a word came to me and only one word. That word was "Integrity." With hope and some trepidation, I wrote that word on a piece of paper and put it in my shirt pocket. In a few minutes JS got up from his knees and I asked him, *"Did you hear anything from the Lord?"* He answered emphatically *"No!"* We chatted a moment and I said, *"Are you certain?"* He said, *"Well, maybe there was something."* I asked him what it was. He said, *"Well, it was just one word."* I said, *"Okay! What was that one word?"* He said it was *"Integrity."*

I quietly pulled out that piece of paper from my pocket trying my best to control my emotions and handed it to him. When he unfolded it and read that single word, this grown man jumped on my couch, on my desk, and shouted and shouted. He had his answer. He would NOT falsify those records.

Surely enough, his employer fired him. Do you want to know what God did that day? He received a call from a Water Management Company and offered him a position of managing multiple cities and their water treatment facilities. Our God is FAITHFUL! HALLELUJAH!

DREAMS, DREAMS, AND MORE DREAMS
by Shawn Scheffler

Genesis 37:5-6 says, "Joseph had a dream, and when he told it to his brothers, they hated him all the more. He said to them, Listen to this dream I had." The story doesn't stop with a dream. In fact, for Joseph, he had another dream. When he shared it with his brothers, they hated him even more and when he shared it with his father, he rebuked him.

With confidence, I will say that at some time or another you've had a dream. The dream was impactful to you. Maybe that dream gave direction in your life or it helped you pursue an idea. I have found that dreams come and they go. However, they are the kind of dreams that you have had when you're asleep. The dreams that Joseph had were not dreams from a pizza he had the night before. The dreams he had were the kind that gave purpose to his life.

The dream I am emphasizing, is the one that God has placed in you to fulfill your destiny and purpose. *Ephesians 2:10 in The Passion Translation* says, *"We have become his poetry, a re-created people that will fulfill the destiny he has given each of us, for we are joined to Jesus, the Anointed One. Even before we were born, God planned in advance our destiny and the good works we would do to fulfill it."*

I can vividly recall the first time God placed His dream for my life in me. I didn't even know at the time that God existed. Yet, I knew it was what I was supposed to do. The dream was to become an author. I wanted to write a book. I was only 9 years old. Just like Joseph, I shared that dream with someone who took what I said and twisted it into something that caused me to avoid that dream for over 29 years.

The dream that keeps you moving forward must be treated with great caution and care. There is nothing more exciting than knowing what you were made to do. Protect that excitement, by developing a strong foundation in your relationship with God. After all, He is the one Who gave you the dream, to begin with. My favorite verses in the entire Bible are found in *1 John 5:14-15*. What stands out to me is that God hears me when I pray His will.

Joseph's story: gives us valuable insight into dreams that are to be pursued. When dreams are from God, they come to pass. We must be careful with who we share those dreams with at first, even those who are closest to us. I've had family members who didn't agree with me becoming an author.

I've had friends who said it just couldn't be done. I've had instructors tell me it was impossible. Each of their comments impacted my life and though I didn't know better at the time, it caused me to delay becoming an author.

Joseph didn't stop dreaming about his dream from the bottom of the well. Those dreams ended up giving him hope in every hopeless situation he faced from that moment forward. *Habakkuk 2:3* says, *"For the vision is yet for an appointed time, but at the end, it shall speak, and not lie: though it tarry, wait for it; because it will surely come, it will not tarry."*

The reason why I said to protect and care for the dream that keeps you moving forward is, for one solid purpose: God gave it to you! When God gives you something—He doesn't take it back. Believe that dream He gave you, for it will sustain you from the bottom of the well to the top spot in your life. Your the one God knew would keep it alive! Go fulfill the dream and purpose for which you were made.

A GENERATION SLIPPING AWAY
by Marcella O'Banion Burnes

I wrote this Dec. 2017 in honor of my aunt and uncle Mr and Mrs Max [Sonny] Munson who helped raise 22 children, 3 sons were natural born. They were the word in action by action.

A generation is slipping away
Do we even recognize what we're losing today?
For ninety year olds and eighties too,
Are a generation that has been through
Things we've heard about, but never knew.
Stories of farms and family life
Of heartaches, war, the depression and great sacrifice.
A harder, but wiser time for sure
Of grim determination to never quit, but endure.
How everyone helped their neighbors and friend.
How they went to war—united to win.
Our shores were protected; they understood,
United, not divided was for our good!
Coming home from church and at the table to pray,
Thanking God for our blessings He gave each day.
Not ashamed to teach the Word of God to their children
And expect them to obey.
Standing for what was right,
Calling sin wrong with all of their might.
This is the generation I grew up under!
Blessed to remember
But; I am left to wonder.
Did I listen closely, will I recall,
All they have taught me.
How to notch a tree to make it fall
Best places to hunt or fish from pa.
Old fashioned butt-switching won't harm you at all.
Or did I learn to bake that cake like ma's?
Precious are these memories
But mostly what I hope left to perceive

Is the godliness and character of these!
I don't know about you my friend,
But I pray we remember and honor them.
An old farm with a creek, rough and ready
but a haven to many.

IS THERE AN EIGHTH DAY FOR SUKKOT THE FEAST OF TABERNACLES?
by Adrienne Gottlieb

First came the blast of the *Shofar* or trumpet to assemble the people and to announce the coming of their atonement. Then *the Day of Atonement* came. At that point the people became cleansed of their sin and were able to fellowship with God. For God, it didn't matter where the people were; in the city or in the field for harvest. He would meet them wherever they were. Therefore, during harvest, the Jews built booths *(Sukkot)* in their fields in order to fellowship with the Lord there. This was a time of great rejoicing, celebration, and fellowship. It was to last seven days. Now, that's a party! By the way, the number seven represents completion. Sukkot therefore is a complete time of fellowship and rejoicing with the Lord.

But then, what does the Lord do? In *Numbers 29:35* the Lord tells us that on the eighth day of gathering, we are not to work again but to hold back or tarry with the Lord.

We are to have a solemn gathering (atzeret). This day is called *Shemini Atzeret*, the eighth day of gathering. Eight is the number of "dedication" in Hebrew. Could it be that since we have heard the Shofar, since God provided the atonement, and since we have celebrated joyously for a week, that we are now to dedicate ourselves to the Lord?

Could it be that God so jealously desires the fellowship of His people that He doesn't want to let us go? In *Zechariah 8:2* the Lord says *"I am exceedingly jealous for Zion. . ."* Does He so want our fellowship that He is unwilling to let us go, and begs us to stay with Him yet another day? The answer is a resounding "yes." His people (in the Old Testament) will not gather again for six months (Passover). Hence, He pleads *"stay longer, be with me, let us worship together."* God will miss the gathering of His people, the music, the festivities, the unity.

One further note of reflection, *Shemini Atzeret* is the eighth day—that is the day after seven. Seven being a perfect number in Judaism, signifies a complete unit of time. Thus, *the eighth day is the day after time.* It is not just the promise of redemption but the actual moment of it. God said, *"Remain with me (atzeret) an extra day,"* a time beyond time. Shemini Atzeret is a taste of the Messianic Age, a time when we are one with God. What greater joy is there than to know we are one with God and that our fellowship with Him is eternal?

~

BELIEVING FOR MORE
by Brandon Stratton

Luke 1:37 tells us that *nothing is impossible with God.*

Many things in life present themselves to be impossible and in the process, cause us to doubt what we carry in Christ. Notice the Scripture says—with God. Too often,we try to overcome life's challenges in and of ourselves. The key here, is our dependence on God. Paul tells us that the great mystery that's been revealed to us is Christ in us, *the hope of glory.* Christ, His anointing and all His finished work is on the inside of us. We also know that all things work together for the good, of those who love the Lord. There is an overcoming power on the inside of you that renders what the world would declare to be impossible as possible today.

> *James 1:2-4 NKJV*
> *My brethren, count it all joy when you fall into various trials, knowing that the testing of your faith produces patience. But let patience have its perfect work, that you may be perfect and complete, lacking nothing.*

James gives us a little insight on how to turn your impossibilities into miracles.

1. *Count it all joy* - When we focus on the end result, and not the circumstance, we receive the God perception; not ours. This allows us to be in joy, knowing the victory is ours. Praise your way through.

2. *Let patience have it's perfect work* - The word perfect here means finished or complete. Enduring faith produces the end result. Let's not disrupt the God plan with our own actions.

3. *Lacking nothing* - I love this... The God plan leaves us lacking nothing.

It's time to tap into your rights, that you possess in covenant relationship with God. It's time, say I can and will walk in 'the more' that God has for me.

~

KEEP YOURSELF FROM FALLING
by Wayne Sanders

2 Peter 1:5-13 KJV
5 And beside this, giving all diligence, add to your faith virtue; and to virtue knowledge;
6 And to knowledge temperance; and to temperance patience; and to patience godliness;
7 And to godliness brotherly kindness; and to brotherly kindness charity.
8 For if these things be in you, and abound, they make you that ye shall neither be barren nor unfruitful in the knowledge of our Lord Jesus Christ.
9 But he that lacketh these things is blind, and cannot

see afar off, and hath forgotten that he was purged from his old sins.

10 Wherefore the rather, brethren, give diligence to make your calling and election sure: for if ye do these things, ye shall never fall:

11 For so an entrance shall be ministered unto you abundantly into the everlasting kingdom of our Lord and Savior Jesus Christ.

12 Wherefore I will not be negligent to put you always in remembrance of these things, though ye know them, and be established in the present truth.

(I will always remind you of these things even though you know them and are firmly established in the truth you now have.)

13 Yea, I think it meet, as long as I am in this tabernacle, to stir you up by putting you in remembrance;

(I think it is right to refresh your memory as long as I live in the tent of this body,)

To keep yourself from falling, take these characteristics that Peter describes, and make every effort to add them to your faith. In order to add anything to our faith, we must hear what God's Word tells us about them. Faith only comes by hearing God's Word.

Someone once asked me, how I stay so strong in the Lord. I was surprised at the question, because I felt pretty weak at that moment. What they saw in me was the Lord's strength, not mine.

When you are struggling with situations, find a brother or sister in the Lord and stay close to them. Find someone that you know who has virtue and the glory of God reflected in their lives; then, listen for Godly council.

Father, I pray for those that are feeling especially lonely today. Bring them a friend to walk with them through tragedies and struggles. For those that are being attacked, I plead the blood of Jesus over their lives and speak victory. Fill them with the undeniable presence of your joy. Bring to them everything necessary to stay strong in you Lord, in Jesus' Name I pray, Amen.

～

THE TRUE STORY OF
GOD'S HEALING POWER
by Bruce A. Higgins

I was running errands in town when I saw a good friend, William David Burris. While getting caught up on things, I asked Bill to play some basketball the next day and he answered, *"Bruce I won't be doing anything for a long time."* He said, *"I was going to call you. I've been diagnosed with a rare type of tumor. They've found a massive growth wrapped on all my vital organs."*

I stood shocked, he said. *"Will you come visit me after they finish running tests before surgery?"* I told him I would. I kept thinking: we're in our early thirties and Bill has a ministry calling.

William was instrumental in my wife and I speaking at the Full Gospel church he attended. One night of that week-long revival, the anointing was so strong, by the Spirit I called Bill out of the crowd saying, *"Bill you have a strong calling by God to not just be a worker for Him, but also to be a strong teacher and minister of His Holy Word."*

When someone has a ministry calling, the devil attempts to stop them before they get started ministering God's Word to others. Just like he did to Jesus, in the desert.

In a few days I went to see him. I had some time to *pray in the Holy Ghost* about it; so, I was ready to minister to him. He told me the latest report was that he had little chance of making it through surgery. The tumor was large, lymphatic, and went all through his body. The doctors were going to do an exploratory surgery, but would probably just evaluate him, do a biopsy, and then just sew him up. They truly felt there wasn't any chance of them doing more than that.

I asked, *"Bill, where is your faith at and what can you believe God for?"* He replied, *"I can't believe like you do, I'm just believing God for my healing. But, I can believe, that when they go in, the whole tumor will be 100% in one place and easily removed."* So we prayed in agreement according to God's Word. *(cf. Mt 19:10)*

It was important to William's healing, that we *agreed in faith* according to what he could believe at that time.

The doctor said the surgery would take an hour and it ended up taking eight. They went to get the biopsy off of William's stomach, but they couldn't find the tumor. They then opened up the entire front and found the mass had attached itself to William's aorta and other organs. The doctors later said, *"We peeled the tumor off of his organs like pulling plastic wrap off of a piece of meat—and we got it all."* Praise the Lord!

While two weeks in the hospital, the devil counter-attacked. In ICU, William was in rough shape, he looked like he was hanging by a thread; very close to death. As I prayed, the *spirit of compassion* came on me and I leaned across his chest and told the devil you're not going to kill him and that William will *live and not die for the glory of God in Jesus' Name.*

It took months for complete recovery. The doctors asked permission to send the biopsy to the University of Michigan Medical Center, because they were not familiar with this type of tumor. William even went there for more tests, which showed no cancer left in his body; therefore, no radiation or chemotherapy was necessary. They told him there were only four cases of this type of tumor in the country.

Today, William David Burris is totally healed and has celebrated 35 years of *God's healing power.*

William, and his wife Susan are Pastors in the United Methodist Church in eastern Ohio. He's just finished his 10th year in ministry, along with all the required schooling. He also recently received the Pastor's Staff of Excellence.

William and his wife now sit on the board of Bruce Higgins Ministries, and for many years have opened up their churches to this ministry. I pray all the healings, salvations, etc. be added to their account before God.

SIGNS WILL FOLLOW
by Ed Marr
The following exerpt was taken from
"FREEDOM IV — Armed and Extremely Dangerous"
▪ Used by Permission.

Signs, wonders and miracles will follow after the saint who refreshes himself daily, since the Lord is working beside him! *(cf. Mk.16:20)*

~

BASIC FAITH SCRIPTURE
by Daryl P Holloman

Proverbs 3:5 KJV
Trust in the Lord with all thine heart; and lean not unto thine own understanding.

Proverbs 3:5 AMP
Lean on, trust in, and be confident in the Lord with all your heart and mind and do not rely on your own insight or understanding.

Hebrews 11:8 KJV
By faith Abraham, when he was called to go out into a place which he should after receive for an inheritance, obeyed; and he went out, not knowing wither he went.

Hebrews 11:8 AMP
[Urged on] by faith Abraham, when he was called, obeyed and went forth to a place which he was destined to receive as an inheritance; and he went, although he did not know or trouble his mind about where he was to go.

Abraham is the Father of our Faith. Abraham is an example as a Father as to how you and I are to walk and live by Faith.

Abraham did not trouble his mind by trying to figure out how God would make His Promise become a living, working reality in Abraham's life.

You and I are to follow Abraham's example and not try to analyze our situation and try to figure out how God is going to move in our circumstances and make His Word a living, working reality in our lives.

Too many times Christians allow their minds to race with seemingly endless thoughts, while their emotions run wild with panic and fear as to the outcome of each possible scenario that bombards their mind, trying to convince them that the worst possible thing is about to happen in their life.

Then they speak negative words, painting bleak pictures on the canvass of their future.

Those negative words are spoken with such conviction; convincing themselves it will happen the way they imagine and causing other people to agree with them.

Proverbs 3:5 is a basic faith Scripture.

We are to trust our Heavenly Father and not waste our time, energy and especially our precious sleep in futile efforts of trying to figure out how the Holy Ghost will bring the Words of Jesus and His Promises in the Scriptures into reality in our lives.

We are to trust Him and Believe His Word and Speak His Word and expect Him to work things out in our lives without you or me trying to work them out or figure out how God will bring His Word to pass.

Even if we did figure it out correctly, the Love of Our Father God would see to it that the Holy Ghost would work it out in an Unexpected Way, just so we would get back on track and Trust the Lord Jesus Christ with All Our Heart and Lean Not to Our Own Understanding.

God Brings His Word to Pass!

Stop Trying to Figure Things Out!

Trust Him!

Obey Him!

Believe Him!

Speak What He Says to Speak!

Do What He Says to Do!

❧

TODAY
by Bill Steinmetz

Today's today
As we wake to the light of a new day dawning.
And find ourselves quietly yawning.
We wander what will happen to us
as this given day comes upon us.
Will is be good or bad,

happy or sad?
If we only knew
we could make it happy or blue.
No matter what comes to us today.
We must take time to softly pray the prayer.
Lord make us all we can be
and let us see like you see.
Okay, so it wasn't the best
but we made it through.
And after all our day was not that bad
neither happy nor sad.
No it was today's today
and another will come we can certainly pray.
After all, your worst today
was the best in a way.
See you were beaten
and wounded for my transgressions
and though it was the worst,
it became the best that I could ever want.
Today's today, tomorrow may never come.

EZEKIEL 22:30
by Jim Andrews

Ezekiel 22:30 KJV
And I sought for a man among them, that should make up the hedge, and stand in the gap before me for the land, that I should not destroy it: but I found none.

I was talking to our neighbor and I asked if he had seen another neighbor that I hadn't seen in a while. I was told the neighbor was in the hospital. He had fallen at work: falling three-stories through a skylight up on the roof, landing on his head on a cement floor. He was taken to the hospital and put on life support. He had been on a ventalator for 90 days and was declared brain-dead. The neighbor stated his family was deciding to pull the plug on the ventalator that very day.

I immediately had a burden of prayer and began to pray until I had a release.

The next day I went over to the [first] neighbor's house to find out if the family pulled the plug, taking the other neighbor off of life-support.

He said the doctors pulled the plug and the family was waiting for him to die, when suddenly he turned his head and said, *"Football."* His life was spared and instead of dying, he went to rehabilitation; now today, he is functioning well and is very grateful that God touched him and let him live. God brought him back to life when he was declared brain-dead and taken off of life-support—to die.

He sent His Word and healed him *(cf. Ps 107:20)*, because someone stood in the gap between life and death, and prayed.

WHAT A MIGHTY GOD WE SERVE!

~

FAITH IS THE KEY
by William Paul Howard

Faith is *the key* to life itself. Without it, one is merely drifting through time with no direction, no purpose, no goals; just existing, even if that.

One has to have faith to even get out of bed in the morning, possibly even to take a breath. Most people go through life, never giving faith a thought; even though they use it every day. I remember reading about a man who walked around holding his head. Because he was sure, that if he let it go, his head would fall off. He was convinced that would happen. He actually had faith. it's just that his faith was in the negative.

I've found, a lot of people have negative faith. You hear them speak it all the time, things like: *"If I went to church the roof would fall in."* Now, no one really expects the roof to fall in, but they believe something bad will happen. Another negative is: *"If I invested in the stock market or anything, I would lose all my money."*

Some people that I have had the unfortunate chance to meet, are so negative; despair and defeat are just dripping off of them. You have to brush the feeling of it off of you when they walk away. The Sun could be out and not a cloud in the sky; yet, they are getting their rain suit ready—confessing that it's going to be a nasty day. We've all encountered people like this in our lives. The unfortunate part is: ***"They just as easily could be positive and smile."*** They could be [and should be] happy the Sun is shining and not a cloud in the sky.

Faith is an *attitude*, it's a *way of life*; good or bad. I prefer to live on the good side of faith. I am convinced that our heavenly Father is concerned about my life; therefore, I ask Him to lead and guide my steps daily. I know I will eat well today and I will eat well again in the future. I will have the things I need; because—I trust in the Lord.

> *Philippians 4:8 KJV*
> *Finally, brethren, whatsoever things are true, whatsoever things are just, whatsoever things are pure, whatsoever things are lovely, whatsoever things are of good report; if there be any virtue, and if there be any praise, think on these things.*

Be positive with your words, things like:

"It's a wonderful day."
"I am going to prosper in the things I invest in."
"I am planting these seeds, and I will have a good Harvest."
"I will excel in my job."
"I am healed."
"I am blessed."
"Everything I put my hand to shall prosper."

Not only Speaking these things but having faith that it shall come to pass.

Be that person who brightens up the breakroom, the office, the meeting room, your home, etc. Become the person they all talk about when you leave the room. It's okay to make them feel a little uncomfortable, because they will notice the change in your attitude and as a result will want to find out what is going on with you.

Faith in God can and will *change your life* and others around you, if you let it.

THE DIVINE INSPIRATION OF SCRIPTURE
by Aaron Jones

Here is some CHRISTIANITY 101 – After your conversion (salvation experience), the absolute first thing you must settle in your mind is:

> *2 Peter 1:20-21 KJV*
> *20 Knowing this first, that no prophecy of the Scripture is of any private interpretation.*
> *21 For the prophecy came not in old time by the will of man: but holy men of God spake [as they were] moved by the Holy Ghost.*

If you don't get this forever settled, you will be knocked around, confused, and led or misled by every doctrine and opinion that comes through town.

This *"Well, that's how you interpret it, but I interpret it this way; this denomination sees it this way... you know everyone has their own interpretation"* IS ALL A LIE FROM THE PIT OF HELL!!! There is one interpretation that is correct (and it is correct in the face of every opinion and circumstance to the contrary) —and that's God's interpretation!

Most opinions, religious ideas, traditions, and doctrines have come from men's pride and human reasoning. God's Word came directly from the Holy Ghost, and it is watched over by the Holy Ghost; in like manner, it will be explained (to you) by the Holy Ghost—if, you will come to it with an open heart. Then make your mind stick with it (stay in study) long enough for Him to work in you, and speak to you.

> *1 John 2:20-21 KJV*
> *20 But ye have an unction from the Holy One, and ye know all things.*
> *21 I have not written unto you because ye know not the truth, but because ye know it, and that no lie is of the truth.*

Notice: he said he's writing to people here that know the truth, and that the Holy Ghost has given them an unction (an anointing to perceive, know, or discern).

Because there are those out there in modern 'churchianity' who teach wrong stuff; like, *false doctrines* and even *doctrines of devils [cf. 1 Ti 4:1]*—they are FALSE ministers (messengers of Satan disguised as angels of light [messengers of truth]) *[cf. 2 Co 11:14-15]*. And if you are not studying your Bible and listening carefully to the Holy Ghost of God—YOU CAN BE DECEIVED!

1 John 2:26-27 KJV
26 These [things] have I written unto you concerning them that seduce you.
27 But the anointing which ye have received of him abideth in you, and ye need not that any man teach you: but as the same anointing teacheth you of all things, and is truth, and is no lie, and even as it hath taught you, ye shall abide in him.

2 Timothy 2:15 KJV
Study to shew thyself approved unto God, a workman that needeth not to be ashamed, rightly dividing the word of truth.

John 10:27 KJV
My sheep hear my voice, and I know them, and they follow me:

John 8:31-32 KJV
31 Then said Jesus to those Jews which believed on him, If ye continue in my word, [then] are ye my disciples indeed;
32 And ye shall know the truth, and the truth shall make you free.

~

NEVER LET PASSION
OVERRIDE PRINCIPLE
by Brian Ohse

The following excerpt was taken from
"THE KEYS TO UNLOCKING THE DOOR OF VICTORY"
■ Used by Permission.

[Speaking of Solomon] But what drew him away from following God? Lust. The Bible says *'he had 700 wives, princesses and 300 concubines.'* ...his hunger for sex, ended up being his destruction. So remember, don't ever let passion overrule principle.

Receive this KEY: *"Your spouse must be of the right spirit, or they will turn your heart away from following Him."*

You know, in writing these things, I'm surprised how bold and direct the Lord is having me be, but time is too short to be playing games. But that's exactly what many churches are doing today. Also, because of this, you're going to see a shaking as never before. Even what we call "mega" churches will collapse from within. I didn't plan on going into this, but apparently there's a purpose. So open your Bible to *Isaiah chapter 5 verse 7.* There's a reason we're looking at this Scripture first, so bear with me. It says, *"For the vineyard of the Lord of hosts is the house of Israel."* You should already know this, but for those that don't, Israel is another word for The Church.

Now let's keep going with this verse, *"and the men of Judah his pleasant plant and he looked for judgment, but behold oppression; for righteousness, but behold a cry."* As you see, I've underlined this particular part, for there's much truth revealed here. But I'm going to present it to you in a way I haven't done, by reading it to you with the words Strong's gave for, "judgment, oppression, and righteousness." For He looked for a place where the people recognized He was worthy to be praised, and that they would support that place with their prayers, and giving if needed.

But instead, all He found was a place of slaughter, where they did nothing but kill the sheep that were under their care. Sheep that were hoping to find a place of moral uprightness, with a minister that would only proclaim the Gospel truth. But instead, they found nothing but those who were weeping and crying out for His Spirit; to fill them. What a powerful truth. Do you see this represents many of the churches today? I tell you, it gets stronger in my spirit every day, that cry for His presence. I pray what I just wrote is breaking your heart enough to cry out to Him to change things. Even if it means closing doors, physical ones. And mark my word, it's going to happen, not because I said it, but because the Word already prophesied it.

I'll show it to you. We're still in chapter 5 of Isaiah, so look at *verse 9, "many houses shall be desolate, even great and fair, without inhabitant."* Now let's look at the connecting *verse 10, "Yea ten acres of vineyard (church) shall yield one bath."* So here you see that the big church will have very little worth. Because "ten acres" represents a large church. Yet there will be no people or even spirit in it. Now the Spirit impresses me to write something I've talked about earlier, apparently this bares repeating. *"There's a lot of people who are hungry for the Spirit, stuck in old dead religious churches with no place to go."* If you agree, then write me and we'll rejoice together that change is coming. ...it must be done *"not by might nor by power, but by His Spirit."* Truly, if the church ever gets a revelation of this Scripture, it will set them free.

∽

HEAL OUR LAND
by Michael Hicks

We are living in dangerous times. The Bible calls it *'the Great Falling Away'* because most of our Christian values are distorted, rejected and replaced with fleshly ideas for daily living. God said this would happen and we should not be surprised by the events of the day. *(See: Matthew 24)* In fact, these events are actually a sign of the return of Jesus the Christ.

The globe is marked with murders, rapes, thefts, sexual immorality, lying and criminal governments; greedy and lustful politicians; divisions at home and in the church; threats if war; lack of compassion; lack of love and even lack of common sense, are ear marks of the return of our

Lord and Savior Christ Jesus. The world is gone astray, and people are like sheep, cows, chicken and pigs going to the slaughterhouse, because they do not know Jesus, or have rejected Him as Lord and Savior. Since the people have *no love for the truth,* God blinds the minds of those who think they are somebody. The foolishness of the world causes them to be futile in their thinking, and as a result their hearts are darkened because of their sinful actions.

So: What do the believers do in these perilous times? The first thing is: we must become *strong in the Lord and in the power of His might.* We need to call things what they are, and quit patty-caking with the truth. When we spend time with the Lord, we allow the Holy Spirit to teach and show us what we must do. We must continue to love the Lord with all our heart and mind, and all of our strength. And continue to love our neighbors as we love ourselves. We need to love those around us, even if they hate us; because we belong to Christ. Remember, we should be desiring to please God and not the world.

> *"If My people who are called by My name will humble themselves, and pray and seek My face, and turn from their wicked way, then I will hear from heaven, and will forgive their sin and heal their land."*
> *– 2 Chronicles 7:14 NKJV*

God gave His children in the Old Testament, and believers in the New, the recipe for Godly living. We need healing from God, we need direction from God, we need wisdom from God; together with, we need our relationship with God to be powerful and filled with love. We must stop being worldly Christians, and start living our lives the way God intended. For this is the reason Jesus came to the earth—to change lives. So we must, if we want to be blessed, humble ourselves, pray to the Father in Jesus' Name, seek God's face instead of His hands, and *repent of our sins or wicked ways and He will heal us and our land. (cf. 2 Chr 7:14)*

~

PRAYING IN THE HOLY GHOST
by Barbara J. White

The *supernatural* provisions God made available to us are to be believed and accessed on a daily basis. The benefits of belonging to the family of God, are boundless!

Just as the body cannot live without eating and drinking; so, the spirit of man *(the new creation)* must be daily sustained through the Word of God and prayer. We are in a divine relationship with God the Father through Jesus the Son and the Holy Spirit. The highest form of prayer is to *"pray in the spirit"* through the power of the Holy Spirit. Paul puts it like this in *1 Corinthians 14:14 AMP, "For if I pray in an [unknown] tongue, my spirit (by the Holy Spirit within me) prays ..."*

The benefits of praying in tongues are boundless! We are receiving more and more *revelation* through supernatural praying. Jude tells us in *verse 20* that *"we build ourselves up [founded] on our most holy faith [make progress, rise like an edifice higher and higher], praying in the Holy Spirit."*

Praying in tongues, enables us to pray the *"perfect will of God"* over every situation. Our minds are limited in knowledge, but the Holy Spirit knows exactly what needs to prayed. We have the privilege of cooperating with Him, and speaking the divine mysteries in tongues.

To pray in tongues, means we are able to build up our spirit-man on our most holy faith. *Faith comes by hearing the Word of God, (cf. Ro 10:17)* but His power is generated in our spirit-man, as we pray in tongues. We can rise higher and higher in the things of the Spirit, and receive revelation knowledge of His Word.

Take time daily, to pray in tongues. Seize every opportunity to pray in the spirit! God has called us to walk in His power and anointing, to be a blessing to a lost and dying world.

"I GET IT!"
COMMUNICATING TO A GENERATION
by Jan Collins

Each generation has its own way of communicating to one another. Phrases, key words, and colloquialisms are unique to each decade of teens and young people. We live in a much different world than we did even twenty years ago, mostly because of technology.

Instead of criticizing the younger generation for having their heads in their iPhones and on social media nowadays, we should build bridges to reach this largest population of unsaved people in the world, if we can just learn how to tap into "their *foreign* language."

Consider the language they use: *"I get it!" "It is what it is!" "Get over it!"* or *"Get over yourself!" "It's all about me!"* and other phrases we (our generation) are probably not even aware of. If you REALLY want to make a difference and possibly affect this millennial generation for Christ, you must learn how to speak their 'foreign' language.

"I Get it!"

Many young people don't know God loves them and that He has a plan for their lives, their circumstances, destinies, and futures.

Setting Scripture to memory, so that we are more relatable is invaluable, because many millennials may not even own a Bible. Besides, no one really wants to be preached to, intimidated or condescended to. Having a Bible app on your phone is good and can help one be more comfortable when sharing. God's Word is anointed and *"sharper than a two-edged sword"* speaking it in a casual conversation can often break *the yoke of bondage*, or a spirit of error off a young person immediately.

"IT IS WHAT IT IS!"

If the young person you are planning to witness or minister to is "un-churched," or never been reared in a church environment, he or she may not know that *Jeremiah 29:11* can be for them individually. So, *"the plans God has for you are for good and not bad—for an expected and successful end"* may be words they have never heard before.

Even their speech can be a game-changer. *"If it is what it is,"* then no one has a chance to be redeemed or be any different than they have always been. God is the only one *'who changes not'* and Jesus is *'the same yesterday, today and forever'*.

But thankfully, we can change our circumstances and our relationship with God by *'not doubting, but believing those things that we say, will come to pass (happen)—and we will have whatever we desire when we pray.'* If we desire a change in ourselves, our hearts or our lives, we must believe our words have power.

Neither our lives nor theirs are set in stone. Many young people are seeking *the supernatural* in the wrong kind of way. The direction of a person's life can change instantaneously in a positive way when they turn and seek God and His Will. There is nothing more instantaneous than becoming transformed into a new creation in Christ. Many young people have lived very dramatic lives. So, the transformation from the old them to the new creation in Christ through a spiritual metamorphosis is definitely—supernatural! Now there's [good] drama for you! *(cf. 2 Co 5:17)*

They may not know who the Apostle Paul was and is, but his story is one of the most quick and dramatic conversion's written in the Bible.

For extended reading: *Jeremiah 29:11; 2 Corinthians 5:17; 2 Timothy 3:16; Hebrews 4:12*

~

FAILURE IS NOT PERMANENT
by Pam Tattershall

There are principles that can be learned in every story recorded in the Bible. The account of partners in fishing, Peter, James and John, found in *Luke 11*, is no exception. Empty-handed from fishing all night, the partners returned to the shore, and began cleaning their nets. Because a large crowd had gathered around Jesus to hear His teachings, He got into one of their boats. Jesus asked Peter to row the boat a little way from the shore, so that He could continue. After Jesus finished, and they returned to shore, He told Peter to cast his nets into the deep. Peter explained to Jesus that their all night efforts had been futile; however, he obeyed and was amazed at the amount of fish that were caught. They became His disciples, and instead of fishing for fish, they became fishers of men *(verses 1-11).* Their past failure was turned around, and they began their lives over with new direction and purpose: Clearly demonstrating that failure is not permanent when you become a follower of Christ.

This particular passage of Scripture is a great encouragement to all who have ever tried something and seemingly failed. Let's look at some principles that we can learn from this passage of Scripture.

• **Be available:** When Jesus had need of a boat, Peter was available to help Him out. Don't be so busy trying to make your own plans work out. Be available for Jesus, to give you new direction.

• **Hear—don't interrupt:** Don't interrupt when Jesus is speaking to you. Interrupting will only cause you to hear only half of what He is saying. Countless times visions, dreams and goals are not fulfilled because we have done our "own thing." All because, we didn't wait to hear the rest of what Jesus was saying to us.

• **Be Obedient:** Peter voiced his concerns to Jesus; however, he didn't allow self-doubt to stop him from being obedient.

• **Be willing to go deeper:** When Jesus told Peter to go into the deep, He didn't tell him how deep to go. The depth of the water into which you and I go depends upon how completely we have cut our ties to past failures or ways in which we have done things in the past.

Allow the Lord to take you deeper, past the greatness of your needs or anxieties about the future. Remember, as with Peter, so it is with us—the fish which represents our visions, our goals, our hopes and desires are to be found in the deep things of God, not the shallow water. We are to go into the deep of God's Word, allowing the Holy Spirit to reveal the greatness of God the Father, in everything that we undertake—even starting again. Failure is not permanent—you can begin anew. This is your New Day.

~

MESSIAH HAS COME
by Molly Sue Allday

Messiah has come to reign in the earth
Yet humbly He came to us at His birth

Sing to the Lord all the earth!
You're matchless in all of Your worth!
He came as a babe, though He is a King
To redeem us to God, so to Him we sing!

Sing to the Lord all the earth!
You're matchless in all of Your worth!

The GOD of the MOUNTAIN II

Ascribe to the Lord glory and strength
Bring gifts to Him, and enter His praise!

Sing to the Lord all the earth!
You're matchless in all of Your worth!
Sing to the Lord all the earth!
You're matchless in all of Your worth!

Great is the Lord, He's worthy of praise
Let all the people rejoice and be glad
Let the fields be jubilant and the trees sing for joy!

Sing to the Lord all the earth!
You're matchless in all of Your worth!

He's coming again to reign over all
No more shall sin and evil prevail
All will give honor and praise to His Name!

We'll sing to the Lord all the earth!
You're matchless in all of Your worth!
Yes, we'll sing to the Lord all the earth!
You're matchless in all of Your worth!

Messiah has come!
Messiah has come!
Messiah has come!
Messiah has come!

ALWAYS
by Steve Farmer

Always!!!!

> *"Now thanks be unto God, which always causeth us to triumph in Christ, and maketh manifest the savour of his knowledge by us in every place."*
> *— 2 Corinthians 2:14 KJV*

This last 12 months have been quite packed with opportunities to give up, throw in the towel, fall out prostrate on the floor, and give in to grief. I've had ample opportunity to scream out *"I cannot bear anymore"*...

I watched my Mom leave this world, found my Dad dead at his home 6 months later, the church was attacked by part of the roof blowing off, both a/c units had to be replaced, the sewer system had to be fixed, the enemy was attacking our people physically, emotionally, and mentally. Our personal home had an a/c unit destroyed, a retaining wall collapsed so that my yard was sinking into a creek, my wife's health was attacked with a vengeance, Satan tried to divide my church, my family, our friends...

Enough of that though... here is the final Word:

My God never left us, kept us in His arms, provided even

more than we needed, let me know Mom and Dad made it safely to His house, sent blessed people to help... everything fixed, hearts full of joy...

WE HAVE TRIUMPHED IN HIM !!!!!!!!!!!!!

～

LET THE SPIRIT RENEW YOU!
by Rachel V. Jeffries

This morning when I woke up, I felt good physically, but my mind was racing like there was something to run from. The funny part is, if I ran away, when I come back the list of things to be completed would still be facing me. I tried to shake it off by making a list. A list usually helps me, but today, it just made it worse. A friend came by and she could tell I was really being tested. Usually I am happy, and we laugh. Today, nothing seemed funny. I don't know if you have ever had this experience or not. My joy tank seemed empty.

She told me, before we got started on my list, we must get rid of being overwhelmed first. We prayed and *spoke to the mountain* of being overwhelmed. Very shortly you could sense the atmosphere change. Even though the list did not get done, getting a couple of things completed sure energized me. I read this week where Lynn Hammond wrote a quote, in it she said, *"Completing of a project gives you energy to complete the next one."* I am not quoting her exactly, but it spoke to me. Some of us are starters but never finish anything. I can tell you finishing is so important to our energy level. Tonight, I am refreshed and ready to go again. Some of the things that seemed too big to deal with, worked out through God putting the item on someone's heart and they met the need.

When we find ourselves being taken by fear, anxiousness, and overwhelming thoughts, we must allow the Holy Spirit to renew us. In *Philippians 4:6* the Word of God says, *be anxious for nothing.* An attitude of gratitude makes the day's cares go away.

Today, I pray, you will allow the Holy Spirit to renew your spirit, and refresh you in body.

> *"And be renewed in the spirit of your mind;"*
> *– Ephesians 4:23 NKJV*

PRAYER: Lord, I come to you with thankfulness for all You have done in my life. When I am overwhelmed, help me to take the time to speak to the mountain looming in my face. Help me to recognize it and allow You to send help to me. Help me to depend on You every day and not do things in my own strength. I love You Lord and thank You for all Your help in every area. I love You, Jesus! AMEN!

CONFESSION: I always trust in the Lord. His praise is continually in my mouth. I speak and sing praises freely. There is not a mountain too big that it cannot be removed by *the power of God* speaking *through* me. I am renewed and have an attitude of gratitude. GLORY!

HOGWASH!
by Mike Harris

The narrative Jesus told in *Luke 15* demonstrates the extravagant love of a Father. It has become one of my favorite lessons on what The Kingdom of God should look like. Most know this as the *"Parable of The Prodigal Son"* although the word, *prodigal* is not in the Scripture. Most of my life the emphasis has been on the bad son, who finally came back home. I never took the time to find out what "prodigal" actually meant. *Prodigal* can be defined as "wasteful" or "extravagant." Jesus is teaching us more about the *extravagant love* of a Father than He is about this wasteful and undeserving younger son. And we can't forget the self-righteous elder son either.

A *Father* has two sons. Let's focus on the Father. And remember that this religious mind-blowing teaching was delivered not only to the disciples, but also to the publicans and sinners. This was in the midst of the Pharisees and Scribes complaining about Jesus hanging out, and even eating with sinners. Oh my! What was Jesus thinking? Perhaps He was showing us that His Kingdom is really about *The Father, prodigal(s)* or *extravagant* (in that he loves two very different sons unconditionally).

What? Hogwash! That is nonsense! And it really is "Hogwash" when we base it on performance and other self-inflicted religious merit systems.

Jesus shows us, that after the younger son wasted everything he had in extravagant sin, which can be considered as "prodigal," he turned toward home. As many of us do, he was seeing himself as unworthy to even be considered a son. His plan was to beg for forgiveness and hope that grace would be given, allowing time to make up for his actions. Sounds like a lot of my past prayers! And as the world's reward system taught him; Surely, he could prove himself worthy of the status of a servant, if only given the chance. [Hogwash!] That is not *grace*. That is not the gift of grace. Please remember, that the Father had been watching and waiting. He drew his robe about himself and ran to pour out his love on his son. When the Father hears a rehearsed plea about being unworthy, etc., he basically proved genuine love with actions that might have sounded like *"Hogwash, nonsense! You are still my son. I love you. Now, go get my son some shoes, a robe, the ring bearing our family rights and let's have a party! Oh, and get that special beef on the grill so we can celebrate! I must now go tell the Good News to your brother. He is a high achiever and doesn't really care much for parties. But he is my son too, and I love him as well."*

∽

NOW HOPE
by Ginny Bridges

In a world ruled by the instantaneous, it's not unusual for us to focus on the now. From online banking, to microwave noodles, we all know that we are urged from every side to do and have everything more quickly.

While it's noticeable in Scripture that God endorses memorials of events from the past, He also instructs us to be mindful of the now. *Romans 8:1* tells us that there is now no condemnation for those who are in Christ Jesus. *Hebrews 11:1* speaks of now faith being the substance of things hoped for, the evidence of things not seen. In the New International Version of *1 Peter 2:10*, we read that at one time we were not people of God, but now we are, having become as living stones. And *2 Corinthians 6:2* tells us that now is the time of God's favor and the day of salvation.

Another favorite [*now*] Scripture is *Romans 15:13, "Now may the God of all hope fill you with all joy and peace as you trust in Him, so you may overflow with hope by the power of Holy Spirit."* Commentaries of this verse stress the all hope, all joy, and all peace benefit of trusting in God. Certainly the all blessings of anything, are abundant and fill our souls to overflowing. In the search for more nuggets of nutrition from this Scripture, let's investigate the [*now*] of His hope, so we may overflow with hope by the power of Holy Spirit.

Now – is defined as currently, presently, at this time. In the passing of time, *now* exists fleetingly. It neither lingers nor hurries; it simply is. *Now* is emphatic, as well as constraining. *"Clean your room now,"* implies that later is not an option, and any delay is unacceptable.

Would we benefit from that understanding of the word *now*? Would our relationship with Jesus be strengthened if we comprehended the significance of *now*? Would our lives look any different if our daily walk reflected a *now* mentality? I think so. It stands to reason that if we were more *now* oriented, we would obey the Lord immediately, rather than procrastinate. The assignments He gives would be completed in His timing rather than our own. The Kingdom of God would be advanced as the harvest is reaped. The Lord challenges me with *now*. He encourages me to refrain from setting and following my own agenda, instead of His.

Hope – is an expectation or desire of something good, an eagerness or anticipation. We look forward to a happy event, an increase of blessing, or the elimination of a negative stressor. *Hope* calls us to be encouraged, to be strengthened, to be revitalized. It gives us a reason to keep on keeping on, to remain steadfast, and to maintain our focus on the goal, the expected end.

Another streak in this lode of golden goodness from God's

Word is this — **Now Hope** is *now*. Presently. **Now Hope** has neither a shame-filled past nor a fear-filled future.

IF ONLY IN MY DREAMS
by Renee Dowling Brophy

If only in my dreams LORD,
I could walk with You
Then that would be the way, LORD
That I'd see it through;
But, Oh with You
Oh with You
All things will win, LORD
Nothing ever fails, LORD
All things will win, LORD
Oh, with YOU.
But, keep me in your heart, LORD
Keep me in your ways
Put your hand in mine, LORD
Lead me all my days......
As this life is shifting
Help me yield to you;
Let my will be bending
LORD, please see me through.
More of YOU
MORE OF YOU
All my days LORD
See me through
With MORE OF YOU.

SPIRITUAL SIGHT
by Michael Nokes

The eyes and ears in the physical, are the primary means by which we interpret or understand information. Yet the Word of God tells us in *Romans 10:17* that our spiritual 'hearing' is opened up supernaturally by the hand of God through his Word (Jesus). Then it states that after our hearing is spiritually opened and we hear the word *'faith'* comes. Therefore *'Faith'* is not something we ourselves gain but it is the gift of God as stated in *Ephesians 2:8*. So that no one has anything to boast about and no one is confused about who gets the Glory. And thus through faith, we are saved by God's Grace.

Hebrews 11:6 states that without faith it is impossible to please him. It states that those who come (or approach) God must believe through Faith that He is, and that he is a rewarder of them that diligently seek him. The truth is a gift to those who seek the Lord. *Isaiah 11:3* states *"And shall make him of quick understanding in the fear of the LORD: and he shall not judge after the sight of his eyes, neither reprove after the hearing of his ears:"* And *Daniel 4:34* states, *"And at the end of the days I Nebuchadnezzar lifted up mine eyes unto heaven, and mine understanding returned unto me, and I blessed the most High, and I praised and honored him that liveth for ever, whose dominion is an everlasting dominion, and his kingdom is from generation to generation:"*

Simply put: HEAR the WORD, SEE the WORD, and then WALK the WORD out. Our flesh wants to believe that the hard part is walking the Word out in our lives. But the hump is still in the middle. It's seeing or understanding or receiving God's revelation that is the difficult part. No matter what you call it, it's He Who gives His children revelation, understanding, a deep knowing, believing and *faith*. So seek Him first, and let Him add all things to you through revelation knowledge of Who He is and—who that makes You!

~

HE MUST BE FIRST
by Landon Roy Wright

Is the desire for your desires, keeping your desires from being fulfilled?

Are the things you want most in life, actually limiting your life right now?

Let's go to the Word for answers.

> *"Still others, like seed sown among thorns, hear the word; but the worries of this life, the deceitfulness of wealth and the desires for other things come in and choke the word, making it unfruitful."*
> *– Mark 4:18-19 NIV*

The desires for things other than the Word, choke the Word. The meticulous details of our life, can choke the Word. This is where it gets interesting.

John 6:63 tells us that, through the Spirit, the Word IS life. When you put all of this together and it can be rephrased like this:

The cares of life choke the true life that is in us.

The life that is in us, the Word, is what makes *everything work together for our good.* When other things become too important in our hearts, that Word is choked for a time. Then it's clear we're not walking in the fullness of who we are in Him; nor of what He has planned for us. That very same abundant life is the foundation of our joy, our strength, and our favor as believers.

As a result we know Who God is, and that the Word says He is good and wants to give us good things. For example, *Psalm 84:11* says *no good thing does He withhold from them that walk uprightly. Mark 11:23-24* says *whatever we desire when we pray, if we believe we've received it, it shall be ours.*

The key is: He has to be No. 1 in our hearts above all these things, and above all these desires.

Speaking from my own personal life, I can testify that when He is first in my heart, good things flow abundantly, but the moment any of those things become too important in my heart, it seems to put the whole process of receiving or advancing on pause.

When He is my main focus, things simply fall into place. But, when the things (or the wants) are first, I hit walls [figuratively speaking]. And the path I'm on—gets more uncertain.

That brings us back to one of the foundational verses for many believers, *Matthew 6:33*:

Seek FIRST, God's Kingdom and righteousness AND THEN all these things will be given unto you.

He MUST be first.

We have to know Him and trust He has a plan *(Je 29:11)*, daily and embrace *the truth* that *our footsteps are ordered (Pr 20:24) by Him.*

TURN THIS SHIP AROUND
by Kim Wear

One of the greatest trials of my life was the death of my husband.

He died 2 days after Christmas 2009. I remember about

45 minutes after he died the kids and I left his room and made our way to the car. I felt great peace like I was in a bubble floating; but, sorrow at the same time. I adjusted the rear-view mirror as I drove out of the parking lot, I could see the window of that room he had just passed in. It was all so surreal.

As we began to drive away, immediately the devil came with those fiery darts that Paul talked about, he was trying to prick the bubble of protection I was in. *"He's gone; What are you going to do now? You can't afford your house, you will never make it! You can't lead a ministry!"*

The peace I was so enjoying, was now being assaulted by enemy forces fighting to steal my future. You see, even in a time like this, the devil never stops being the devil and he never tells you something you couldn't believe about situations, he only tells you stuff you could actually believe. It was then, the Holy Spirit spoke to my heart, *"You better turn this ship around."* I knew exactly what the Holy Spirit meant by those words.

He was talking about the tongue being like the rudder on a ship, as mentioned in *James 3:4.* The ship is our life and the words are the rudder. In life, the words you speak, determine the direction of your life. Even though I didn't feel like it, I had to fight the fight of faith: I had to use my authority and make my words line up with the Word of God in order to create a new life, and a new normal for my children.

So I spoke up and said, *"Kids, you know what we are going to do? We are going to go on. Everything is going to be alright."*

I spoke to the younger kids that had dreams of playing ball, being an artist, going into the military. etc. It wasn't just my future at stake. I told each one they could go forward and do those things because God was with us. He needed me to set the course of my life. If I kept listening to the enemy I would have been shipwrecked. And just like the rudder of a ship determines the direction of the voyage; words may not cause you to arrive at the destination immediately, but they head you in that direction. And eventually, if you continue to speak the Words of God in that direction—you will arrive there.

[Let me repeat.] Even though *I didn't feel like it, I had to fight the fight of faith.* I had to *use my authority* and *make my words line up with the Word of God*; thereby, creating a new life for me and my children.

Today my children have set sail in their own adult lives, doing very well, some married; but all living for God. I set the course for my own ministry, I went out 5 weeks after my husband's death, traveling all over the nation preaching:

VICTORY IN THE NAME OF JESUS!

TWO SIDES TO EVERY STORY
by Heather Wright

There's always two sides to every story. In the Bible, Jesus had one story and the Pharisees had another. Only the Pharisees' version was made up of false accusations. If you ever want to know the truth about anything and everything, ask Jesus, our Abba Father.

> *"I am THE WAY, THE TRUTH, and THE LIFE.*
> *No one comes to the Father except through me."*
> *— John 14:6b NKJV [caps added]*

Darkness has to bow to *the light* every time.

Last year, the Lord clearly spoke to me and told me that I couldn't fix a particular situation. He told me that I just needed to let it go and give it to Him. For so long, I felt like I couldn't let go. Not because I enjoyed dealing with these particular issues, but for some reason, I felt obligated. Because of this one situation, I had never had peace in this area of my life.

The reason I didn't have peace, was because I had to be willing to completely surrender to Him. But I was too concerned what others' opinions about me would be, when the Lord's opinion is the only one that really matters. After many years and much prayer, I was able to finally let go. For the first time in my life, I have more peace than I ever knew was possible.

Come to me, all you who are weary and burdened, and I will give you rest. Take my yoke upon you and learn from me, for I am gentle and humble in heart, and you will find rest for your souls. For my yoke is easy and my burden is light. – Matthew 11:28-30 NIV

Nothing is worth giving up your peace. I have learned over the years, to *follow peace.* Peace always leads me closer to Jesus, because *God is love* and He is our peace.

Peace I leave you; my peace I give you. I do not give to you as the world gives. Do not let your hearts be troubled and do not be afraid. – John 14:27 NIV

THE RACE
by Michael Hicks

Our Christian lives have been compared to a race. Placing first, second, or third, doesn't matter in this particular race. What does matter, is finishing the race. All children of God are involved in this race, or this trek toward eternal life. Every born again believer is equipped with a talent, a gift and God's anointing to finish this race; but, it is up to us to run it.

To run this race, we must be obedient to the Word of God. We must be faithful, authentic, and truthful as we journey through this life serving the *true* and *living God*. When we walk in the love of God, we are actually running the race with grace (God's divine influence upon the hearts of men). When we love our brothers and sisters in Christ, we are running the race. When we pray for our enemies, we are running he race. When our Bible speaks to us, we are in the race. This race is not always smooth, but we have the power through Christ Jesus our Lord to overcome all obstacles, circumstances and fiery darts that may come our way.

As we run this race there are things we have to do.

> *Let us lay aside every weight, and the sin which so easily ensnares us... – Hebrews 12:1b*

When we lay our flesh aside, and every sin aside we can easily run the race. When we can say no to the things we used to do and embrace the Word of God in our everyday lives, the finish line will become a reality in our lives. If we call ourselves a Christian and we are still chasing after sex, getting high or drinking, hating one another, gossiping, lying on anyone, stealing, cheating, beating and fighting one another. Or if we are serving someone other than Jesus, we will become ensnared with these stumbling blocks (or weights) and won't be able to finish the race God has planned for us.

> *Let us run with endurance the race that is set before*

us, looking unto Jesus, the author and finisher of our faith... – Hebrews 12:1c.

As we run this race with endurance, stamina, fortitude, and patience, we should keep our eyes on Jesus, the Christ. We should be focused on His way of doing things and not our's. We should be intent on abiding in Him, and allowing the Holy Spirit to guide us in this race. There are many, many, enemies of the Gospel, and if we are not focused, or if we are dabbling in sin, our race could be lost.

EUROCLYDON
by Ruth Tatum

The Apostle Paul, a prisoner of Julius, the centurion had entered a ship sailing for Italy. After many days, they came unto 'the Fair Havens' near the city of Lasea. Paul warned the ship's captain that he perceived the voyage would suffer hurt and damage, not only of the freight, but of their very lives. However, they did not believe him, and chose rather to depart and spend the winter in Phenice.

The south wind blew softly, so they pulled anchor and sailed close to Crete. But shortly after, there arose a tempestuous wind, called *Euroclydon*. The winds were so strong that they had to let the ship drive herself. They came near Clauda, and undergirded the ship, but the next day, the winds were so violent, they began throwing the freight overboard.

After many days with no Sun or stars, all hope that they would be saved was gone. But, Paul stood in the midst of them saying, *"Sirs, you should have listened to me, and not left Crete, rather than to have suffered this harm and loss; but now, I want you to 'be of good cheer,' for no one will lose his life, but only loose of the ship. Because tonight, the Angel of God, whose I am and who I serve, said, "Fear not Paul, you must be brought before Caesar, and God has given you all them that sail with you, none will die. We will be cast upon an island."* After 14 days and nights, they cast anchors out and were about to flee from the ship; when Paul told the centurion that unless they stayed in the ship, they couldn't be saved. They had gone fourteen days without food, so Paul told then to eat. They broke bread, blessed it, they ate and regained strength.

Paul assured them again, that they would not die. There were 276 men on board the ship, and they began to cast the wheat into the sea. The next day, they took up anchors, loosed the rudder, and sailed toward shore; thus, running the ship aground. The back part of the ship was broken because of the waves of the sea. The soldiers counsel was to kill the prisoners, but the centurion wanted to save Paul, so he told all that could swim to jump in and make for the shore. Those who could not swim used boards and broken pieces of the ship to go on, but they all made it to land safely.

As Christians, we all go through some storms in our life; and like Paul and the ship's crew, we are tossed to and fro, we are bruised and broken by the overwhelming waves of life's sea. We [at times] feel like all hope is gone; there's no way to escape the destruction Satan has attacked us with. But even if all hope is gone in the natural, if we will call unto the God of the supernatural, He will reach down and rescue us before we go down for the third time. He won't let us drown in Satan's cesspool of disappointments. He will set us on higher ground and restore to us, all the things that were broken. Many times in these attacks, we need to get rid of some stuff; throw some things overboard, that are weighting us down. Things that are holding us back, just out of reach of the victory. If we will *'lighten the load'* and give all this excess baggage to Jesus, we can stay afloat and drift on into the Fair Havens of his rest.

ALMOST THERE
by Wayne Sanders

I have some very good news for you today. You are almost there. How do I know this? Just before you receive the thing that God has promised, it seems like all the forces of darkness come in a direct attack against you. But don't be alarmed or be shaken by all this.

Luke 6:47-49 NKJV
47 "Whoever comes to Me, and hears My sayings and does them, I will show you whom he is like:
48 He is like a man building a house, who dig deep and laid the foundation on the rock. And when the flood

arose, the stream beat vehemently against that house, and could not shake it, for it was founded on the rock. 49 But he who heard and did nothing is like a man who built a house on the earth without a foundation, against which the stream beat vehemently; and immediately it fell. And the ruin of that house was great."

Your strength is developed by practicing and applying the Word of God that you hear. This will cause you to grow and to mature. As you develop into a man or woman of God, you will develop a lifestyle of believing that God can and will do the impossible through you.

Hang on tight! Don't give up too quickly! Help is on the way. The Bible is our ultimate source of encouragement.

Father, we are ready to walk into any situation, as long as you are with us. We know that we can do anything when Christ is our strength. Thank you for Your Word that brings comfort and peace, in Jesus' Name.

Psalm 46:1-3, 7 KJV
1 God is our refuge and strength, a very present help in trouble.
2 Therefore will not we fear, though the earth be removed, and though the mountains be carried into the midst of the sea;
3 Though the waters thereof roar and be troubled, though the mountains shake with the swelling thereof. Selah.

7 The Lord of host is with us; the God of Jacob is our stronghold. Selah.

Blessings on the journey, and remember, the best is yet to come. So look for it.

~

COMPANION ON MY JOURNEY
by Marilyn Neubuaer

It was a lovely summer evening in 1983 when I had a companion on my journey. I was living in Broken Arrow, Oklahoma while working at the City of Faith Hospital in Tulsa which was founded by Oral Roberts. A friend who lived in Claremore, Oklahoma, had invited me to come and spend the day with her on Saturday.

My plans were to go early in the morning and then return home late afternoon before dark. However, we were having such a good time, she asked me to stay a little longer and have supper. We had a delightful time, but soon I realized it was later than I thought and I needed to start for home.

From Claremore it was a little over an hour and a half drive back to where I lived in Broken Arrow. After coming through the toll road I decided to get off the highway and take a short cut, putting me on a country road which would save me around 20 minutes. Once I got on the country road, I realized it was probably not the best decision since I was all alone after dark. The moon was hidden behind the clouds making it very dark with no stars in sight.

I often talk to the Lord when I'm driving alone. This evening was no exception. Thinking I had not made the best choice in getting off the toll road, I said. *"Lord, it is really dark out here tonight!"* Having just spoken those words a helicopter flew above my car. The pilot turned on his spotlight, illuminating the road directly in front of my car. This light continued to shine, guiding me all the way across the country road. As soon as I arrived at the main street in Broken Arrow, the helicopter turned upward into higher skies.

The word *'accompany,'* means a companion on a journey. As all of this was happening, I became aware that God had assigned my guardian angel as my companion on the journey.

There are angels surrounding us at all times. We don't see them, but we can encounter angelic assistance in time of need. Develop an awareness that God gives His angels charge over each one of us to accompany, defend and preserve.

For He will give His angels [especial] charge over you
to accompany, defend and preserve you in all your ways
[of obedience and service].
— Psalm 91:11 AMP

FORGIVENESS
by Michael Nokes

Brother Jeff, a church leader who led my son Michael Noah to the Lord, spoke about forgiveness on the phone. He gave no detail, but he didn't need to. The Holy Spirit let me feel the depth of his words. The Holy Spirit gave his words life. In an instant, I heard and received from the Lord.

Praying the next morning, before having my coffee mind you, I spoke words of forgiveness. I wanted them to be deep words, I needed them to be deeper, more sincere than ever before. My heart desired to obey my Father. When I repeated my words, *"Heavenly Father, I forgive her completely,"* the Holy Spirit snapped the words, *"Act like it!"* It wasn't harsh but it was quick. I was startled. I stopped everything. He then showed me the prodigal son's father with his arms open wide, receiving his son. There was no resentment in his heart, only love for his son. As I took these things in, I began to sob. His Dad treated him the opposite way his brother felt like he deserved. His Dad's heart was pure in forgiveness and love toward his son. The intake was painful. I sobbed at the realization that I may have never forgiven in completeness.

Punishment in any form means that forgiveness did not take place. *"Vengeance is mine,"* says the Lord. Stand for the things of God, but rest in Him to set things right. We can do all things through Christ who strengthens us! God knows the desires of your heart. We should pay attention to His. It's not about anyone else; it's about me and Him. It's about love. It's about trust. It's about obedience. It's about my walk with Him. He is a rewarder! He repays both sides when we suffer for Christ.

~

CHILD-LIKE FAITH
by Aaron Jones

"The overnight snow was Tulsa's first since **0.5 inch fell Dec. 17, 2016.** Tulsa recorded 3 inches of snow in 2016, including 2.5 inches on Jan. 9." - *excerpt from the Tulsa World, Jan 7, 2017*

That Dec. 17, 2016 date, just happened to be my youngest daughter's 14th birthday.

She prayed and believed God that it would snow on her birthday; continually telling us and everyone else (grandparents, cousins, friends, store clerks, etc.), that it would snow on her birthday. Several times she repeated the same confession, *"I asked God for it to snow on my birthday, and it will snow; just watch."*

Well, it did! As a matter of fact, it was one of only two snowfalls we had the entire 2016/2017 Winter here in Oklahoma, and the only snow we received in our community.

Think about that. It wasn't much, [just a good dusting], but it was snow, and it was the only one we had, and—it happened on her birthday!

> *Mark 10:15 NLT*
> *I tell you the truth, anyone who doesn't receive the Kingdom of God like a child will never enter it.*

This year she prayed for something much more important. This December (2018), she told us a family member who, along with their spouse and children that had been separated from all of the rest of the family over a misunderstanding, would be coming home before the holidays.

Once again, she kept saying it, over and over; purposely making the confession, "_____*will come here before Christmas. I asked God for them to come home, and* _____*will walk in this house, Just watch, God is going to bring them home.*"

When other family members stated that would take a miracle, my daughter's answer was, *"Well duh, isn't that what Jesus does—miracles?"* She would not back off what she was believing God for. She was determined this would happen just like she had prayed.

On Christmas Eve, much to everyone's surprise (except my daughter's) _____walked in our house, sat down and visited quite a while with us; my daughter would not leave their side. That evening _____returned with their spouse and children to join us for dinner and more fellowship.

Since that time, much with this family member and the rest of our family has been restored.

Understand, this person and their spouse are great people, and the other members of our family they had the misunderstanding with are also great people. But the devil wants to divide and tear-up families, and he was working in this to wound and hurt everyone involved.

But God, [because of the child-like faith of a 16 year old girl] stepped into the situation, and it is now well on the way to being completely mended.

It was Isaiah that said, *"...a little child shall lead them,"* speaking of creatures in Heaven. Actually, God's Word has much to tell us about children. And the fact is, the more I watch them... the more I am convinced children have much to tell us about God, if we would only listen.

OBEDIENCE BRINGS BLESSINGS
by Paul Thomas Adams

I help out at "Lavern's Wedding Chapel" in northeast Oklahoma when her minister is sick or out of town. I had not heard from Lavern's in weeks and was trying to find things to do in between rounds of chemo, and navigating being retired before I was ready. What to do today, put on my trusted khaki shorts, hikers and printed tee and head to the pawn shop to see what was new in used guns and knives, also a good place to tell a questionable tale or two without being called out on it; normal old guy behavior. I was setting on the edge of my bed my wife was putting out my clothes for me to wear, yes, I know, shame on me and yes, she is the best. She commented that I looked bewildered or unsure about something, I told her my brain keeps telling me to wear those faded overalls, tee shirt and my new balance sneakers. She pointed out they were almost bleached white and had several holes around the knees, why these? I know, I said. Maybe God is going to put me on some dirty work today, ha, ha, I hope not I'm tired. So, faded "holy" overalls, tee shirt, well-worn new balance cross trainers, I was ready for fence row work or something akin.

I was sitting in my truck in the pawn shop parking lot, which happens to be two doors down from the wedding chapel. I jumped out of my skin when someone pounds on my window, it's Patricia from the chapel, come to the chapel with me and do a wedding right now. I said what, *"Do you see what I'm wearing?"* Doesn't matter, she said, I can't find the preacher and they've driven from Wichita and have been waiting an hour. I told them I saw you drive by, but you weren't dressed up, they said fine, they were ready to go back home. I apologized for the way I looked, and the young bride said I was perfect, and she cried all through the ceremony. After I pronounced them, she hugged me and sobbed for at least a whole minute, then went to the ladies room, what happened I asked, the groom said, God showed up, that's what happened. They had planned a church wedding in Wichita, with her father giving her away, but he had passed from a heart attack three weeks previous, so they had eloped to ease the pain. He said when we saw you we both lost it, her dad was 60 years old, light beard, 6' 1" 350 lbs and could be found any day of the week in faded overalls, tee shirt and new balance sneakers! Oh I forgot to tell you, I'm 61 years old, 6' 1" 340 lbs and now you know the rest, I'm glad I was obedient and changed clothes before leaving the house, so he could bless us both.

~

TOTAL HEALING
by Brian Ohse
The following excerpt was taken from
"THE KEYS TO UNLOCKING THE DOOR OF VICTORY"
▪ Used by Permission.

Now receive total healing, from the very crown of your head to the tips of your toes. Holy Spirit, wash them afresh in the blood of the Lamb; Amen. Now go forth in His anointing, power and glory, and set the captives free. Now let's look at the second Scripture that goes along with this truth. Turn to Exodus chapter 5 the last part of verse 16, "behold thy servants are beaten; but the fault (or problem) is in thine own people (or leaders). Does that clarify any doubt you might have had? So another key: is recognizing your leadership ability, and walking in it.

Now let's [look at] the word "Eli." Understand, this I'm speaking about, I didn't know what I would uncover. But once again you'll see the reason and will agree with what's said. Listen to what the church has become according to Strong's terminology; "Eli" gave just one word, "lofty" and when this word was studied in Webster's, we come up with "pompous, arrogant, and haughty." Does that describe the church today? But hold on, the Spirit impresses me to go deeper; I'm to research the word, "pompous." Listen to these words, then cry out to God for His bride to be changed. "Exaggerated show of dignity or self-importance; pretentious." But the truth is to be made even more clear. How? By looking at the definition for "pretentious," listen to what Webster's said, "claiming or demanding a position of distinction or merit; especially when unjustified."

Now will you fall to your knees and cry out to God in the churches' behalf? Do you think I am being a little to hard on the church? I have to admit sometimes I wonder myself. Is this really the state of the church in general? I can say yes with a sad confidence. How? Because only yesterday I was impressed to read to a neighbor [what I had been writing] and her response afterwards? I'm right on track. She said what you spoke is exactly right. She said, *"There's no doubt in my mind that you're in the right place for this purpose."* She said, *"I'm Baptist."* Then I said, *"The church has taught you to do nothing but manipulate people,"* she agreed. Then I spoke to her husband about some specifics, then he said, *"all churches do is talk about money,"* he said, *"they are more concerned about their Lexus than they are the people."* Boy, talk about a truth hitting home! Yet, the couple are looking for a place to fellowship and grow. But, where can I tell them? Truly people are hungry for the Spirit of God.

THE KINGDOM
by Adrienne Gottlieb

One of the first things Jesus tells us, is to repent and believe in *the Good News,* because the Kingdom of God is at hand *(See: Mk 1:15).* What is this Kingdom? How do we recognize it?

While some say the Kingdom of God is in the future, others say it is today. Some believe it is allegorical, others see it as literal. Some even see the Kingdom as fulfillment of the promises God made to the Jews, while others believe it has nothing to do with the Jews! Some believe it pertains only to Heaven, and yet others believe the Kingdom has an earthly presence. Nevertheless, The Kingdom is the singular most talked about subject by Jesus in His earthly ministry. You'd think we have a clearer picture. Let's see how the King, Himself, described it in His parables.

- The Kingdom needs to be planted *(Mt 13:3)*
- There are outside influences that can affect the Kingdom *(Mt 13:5-7)*

- The Kingdom yields a crop *(Mt 13:19)*
- There are enemies to the Kingdom *(Mt 13:24-30)*
- The Kingdom grows in the midst of problems *(Mt 13:26)*
- There is a time when the enemies of the Kingdom will be destroyed *(Mt 13:30)*
- The Kingdom grows and nourishes others *(Mt 13:31-32)*
- The Kingdom of God is infectious *(Mt 13:33)*
- The Kingdom of God is priceless *(Mt 13:44-45)*
- The Kingdom of God is joyous *(Mt 13:44)*
- There is a time when the fullness of the Kingdom will be revealed *(Mt 13:48-50)*
- There are people who labor in the Kingdom *(Mt 20:1-16)*
- There is grace and compassion in the Kingdom *(Mt 20:1-16)*
- Contracts are made in the Kingdom *(Mt 20:13)*
- There is generosity in the Kingdom *(Mt 20:15)*
- What one does in the Kingdom is more important than what one says *(Mt 21:28-31)*
- Sometimes people do not recognize the Kingdom *(Mt 21:33-40)*
- There is a time for punishment in the Kingdom *(Mt 21:40)*
- There is celebration in the Kingdom *(Mt 22:2)*
- People are invited into the Kingdom *(Mt 22:3)*
- Not all people will accept their invitation into the Kingdom *(Mt 22:3-8)*
- You have to be dressed a certain way to come into the

Kingdom—clothes of righteousness *(Mt 22:12)*
• In the end, few are really chosen to enter into the Kingdom though many are called *(Mt 22:14)*

The Church (the people of God) is the visible manifestation of the Kingdom of God. How are we doing? Can those outside the Kingdom recognize us as subjects of The King? You decide.

THE SILENT SURPRISING VOICE
OF THE SAVIOR
by Len Blanchard

One morning I received a call from a mother about her daughter, L C. She was in the hospital in ICU. The family had been called in. The mother asked me to come to see her daughter.

When I arrived, I went in the ICU room alone. L C was not able to speak and was near death. I took her by the hand and prayed for her. There was no special presence of God that I could sense.

As I walked out to the waiting area to see all the family, the mother came up to me and said, *"What do you think, Brother Len?"* Without hardly taking a breath I said, *"Ah, she will go home tomorrow."*

If I have ever wanted to take back some words it was those. I was so embarrassed, I hardly spoke to the family. I offered a prayer and left. Well, within the hour I received an excited phone call from L C's sister. She told me that L C had woke, set up on the side of the bed, and was going home the next day.

I cannot explain how I felt on that day. The tremors in my body were like little shock waves. The Silent Surprising Voice of the Savior spoke loudly to me in those moments.

TODAY IS NOT YESTERDAY
by Mike Harris

Consider how we are able to use the same seven names for the days of the week, the same twelves names for the month of the year, the same numbers for the hours; yet by changing a single digit we have no problem believing that today is a new day. TODAY IS NOT YESTERDAY.

Yet we seem to somehow allow our yesterdays to define our tomorrows. The moment we receive Christ as our Lord, and accept His *gift of grace through faith* in the works He already accomplished, we become *new creatures*. It is no longer I, but it is *now* Christ. The former me is dead, gone and past; yesterday is gone. *"Therefore if any man be in Christ, he is a new creature: old things are passed away; behold, all things are become new."* – *2 Corinthians 5:17 KJV*

Old things are passed, and now, all things are new. The past, [and we all have one] is where we have a tendency to remember our past victories and try really hard to forget the failures. Both categories of our past, seem to get placed in a permanent file, conveniently located, so that future reminders and references by ex-spouses, ex-friends (the unfriended FB folk), and ex-bosses can easily retrieve them to ensure continued payments are being made. Our religious mind-sets often follow the same path, but only with a spiritual slant.

We cannot right the wrongs of the past; but Christ can and He did! This is an absolute transformation that cannot happen apart from Christ. Our spirit man has been reconciled according to God's promise, *the same Spirit that raised Christ from the dead,* lives in every *new creature in Christ*—this is a done deal!

Therefore, we should no longer subject ourselves [today] in Christ, to our [yesterday] without Christ. *Today,* with Christ we are able to live in the newness of His grace. We are able to live *justified* according to—*the finished work of the cross.* We are called, glorified and being conformed to His image. Today is not yesterday. The old life is gone; a new life has begun! And you can believe that!

~

IF YOU WILL HEAR MY VOICE
by Aaron Jones

The crazy things we say (and evidently think) to try and justify our disobedience (sin), e.g., *"God knows my heart,"* *"That's not what we are doing with it"* and *"Now we are living under grace"* or there's my personal favorite, *"My church/Pastor says it's okay."*

Yet, none of these excuses would work in a Court of Law anywhere in the world. IMAGINE! *"Yes judge I realize some feel that way about cocaine...but that's not what we use it for at our house." "That's true your Honor, but you know me, I'm not a criminal, I'm a good person, you know my heart..."* —are you kidding?

Why would we think these kind of lame 'religious' excuses will work as a free pass for our crimes (disobedience) against God?

God gives us **"An invitation to obey and participate"** in His plan. He simply ask that we hear His Voice: *"Today, if you will HEAR MY VOICE?" "My sheep HEAR MY VOICE...", "Behold, I stand at the door, and knock: if any man HEAR MY VOICE..."*

But sadly, man often CHOOSES to not hear so clearly; we tend to put our own little twist on everything God says.

- GOD SAYS paint it blue, and WE THINK blue-green would look better.

- GOD SAYS don't touch it, but WE THINK since it looks good, a little bit will be okay.

- GOD SAYS this is bad—evil, but WE THINK our good intentions will somehow make it acceptable.

- GOD SAYS support 'that' financially, but WE THINK I have to take care of 'this' so I will just pray for that.

Like Adam and Eve, people hear THE VOICE OF GOD moving where they live and [since we got it all covered] they ignore Him or even hide from Him.

> *Genesis 3:8 KJV*
> *And they heard THE VOICE OF THE LORD God walking in the garden in the cool of the day: and Adam and his wife hid themselves from the presence of the LORD God amongst the trees of the garden.*

See the WISE MAN built his life on the Word of God, he heard The Word and obeyed it. He applied it to his everyday activities. But the FOOLISH MAN failed to act on what he heard and everything he built, (his life's work) was lost; as if on sinking sand. *[Mt 7:24-27]* How sad!

I'll tell you exactly why some folks are not blessed, they simply are—not listening.

Deuteronomy 28:2 KJV
And all these blessings shall come on thee, and over-
take thee, (IF) THOU SHALT HEARKEN UNTO
THE VOICE OF THE LORD THY God.

Isaiah 1:19 KJV
(IF) ye be willing and OBEDIENT, ye shall eat the
good of the land:

LISTENING requires attention (to every detail), this takes study, prayer, cleaning all the 'religious' wax out of your ears and mind, it takes diligence, sacrifice (of your time, plans, personal opinions and agendas). It takes being around God's mature ministries WHO HEAR FROM GOD, so that you gain insights and experience how God speaks and moves.

We must be like little Samuel when he said to the Lord, *"Speak; for thy servant heareth."* [1 Sa 3:10] He then (even fearful) shared WHAT GOD TOLD HIM and corruption was exposed at the highest levels in the temple and removed. The people were pointed back to God, Kings were anointed and a nation was impacted forever.

Now, it's our turn Church. GOD IS SPEAKING—Rise Up Church!

DEVELOPING A
"HEALTHY DON'T CARE"
by Landon Roy Wright

To piggyback off of my previous article, the Lord has helped me develop what I call a "healthy don't care."

See, in secular society, the phrase *"I don't care"* is often affiliated with indifference, sometimes laziness or grumpiness, perhaps low ambition, maybe even depression and things of that category. More often than not, it has a negative connotation.

Before I got filled with the Holy Spirit 10 years ago, that was me and many of those words could describe me then. I didn't care too much about anything. Not to be super negative, I just kind of went with the flow and didn't really have much vision for my life or faith to change it. Like many non-believers, I began to settle for a life that I didn't truly want in my heart, but at the time I believed that was the best I could do.

Since then, the Lord has worked in me to where those descriptors don't describe me at all today. In fact, the Lord has grown me to expect nothing short of a life of excellence and my heart's desires fulfilled. Sometimes maybe so much so, that I can stress myself out striving for certain outcomes and accomplishments, waiting for the answered prayers to manifest. In today's high-anxiety society, it's almost like if something isn't perfect or the absolute best in its category, then it has no value at all.

This is a lie of the enemy of course, but the enemy is real and he has a tendency to try to make us feel that way. Afterall he is the accuser of the brethren *(Revelation 12:10)*, the father of lies *(John 8:44)*, and the god (little 'g') over the world system *(Ephesians 2:2; 2 Corinthians 4:4; 1 John 5:19)*.

Sometimes I can be striving so much for perfection and excellence, that I miss the days when I was careless and just went with the flow, but I have too much Word in me now to live that way, because I know it's a foolish approach to life and I know I won't get a single day back.

Regardless of any outcome, or how good of a game I coach, how good of a class I teach, how good of a job I do. No matter how eloquent I sound or how great I get my point across, God is still God and God is always good and life goes on. The sun is going to come up tomorrow and guess what?

Our footsteps are STILL going to be ordered by the Lord (Psalm 37:23).

He works out ALL things to the good of those who love them and are called according to His purpose (Romans 8:28).

He will STILL supply ALL of our needs according to His riches and glory (Philippians 4:19).

Knowing that the cares of this life choke the Word *(See: Mk 4:18-19)*, I try not to hold on too tight to anything but Him, because He alone is the source.

He is the vine and we are the branches. We have to remain in Him to produce fruit, and when we follow Him, things will flow. Don't let the cares of this life stop that flow! Don't strive too hard and lose sight of Him!

So that's what I call a healthy "don't care." Truthfully, most of the time I do care, and I do still plan on pursuing excellence once I finish this article, but if there's ever one second, or minute, or hour, or day, or month, or year, of falling short of it. Guess what? Nothing matters, compared to knowing Him *(Philippians 3:8)*! None of it!

Besides, God is the promoter, not man *(Psalm 75:7)*. That includes us. We can spend ourselves on Him or on our work, but He decides when to take us further. So let's keep our hearts at rest and full of joy, don't let any of these cares snatch any of it.

The GOD of the MOUNTAIN II

❧

HOMELESS
by Marcella O'Banion Burnes

*(In memory of Krystal B. Who died in pedestrian accident
while living on streets in a city in Texas)*

Homeless
They are vanishing before our eyes into thin air
Right the wrong
"Christian"
Do You care?
Needless suffering on our streets
Homeless dying on corners that we meet
I'm hungry, they do cry
Lonely, scared, tired, hopeless they die.

"CHRISTAINS"
Marching on Calvary's Road
Staunch believers of the Word
Paths cross in the streets
Will you their needs meet?
Glancing quickly we hurry by
Guilty, while in our warm beds we lie

JESUS came for these, *the lost*
The sinners, the addict, the dealer
The hopeless, at all cost

He fed the five thousand

Three, one day too
With JUST ONE on a street corner
What will you do?

~

PRAYER KILLERS
by Michael Hicks

Even though prayer is a powerful component in our Christ life, there are some hindrances to prayers we need to be aware of.

> *If I regard iniquity in my heart, The Lord will not hear. – Psalm 66:18*

If we are practicing sin in our lives, our prayers will not be answered, unless it is the prayer of repentance or forgiveness. God will not hear the prayers of sinners. If I am a thief or a liar in my heart and going to God in prayer, my prayers will not be heard by God. If I am practicing sexual immorality in my heart and pray to God, the skies will be like brass and God will not hear my prayer. If I am cheating my brother or coveting my sister or gossiping, backbiting and hating others in my heart, God will not hear my prayer. If I am committing adultery physically or spiritually in my heart, God will not hear my prayer. In fact the only prayer God will hear is a prayer of repentance or a prayer of forgiveness.

You ask and do not receive, because you ask amiss,
that you may spend it on your pleasures. – James 4:3

God will not answer selfish prayers. He will not answer your prayer for your neighbor's spouse, He will not answer prayer for a new car for you to take pride in, and He will not bless you with a big house for you to boast to your friends, He simply will not answer selfish prayers. He will answer prayers from the heart, for the good of His Kingdom.

There are thousands, it if not millions of people in gambling casinos and race tracks, praying to Jesus to get rich. They call on the Name of Jesus, as they pull the one-armed bandit, in hopes He will bless them for a hit. There are people who have visions and will enact a scheme and plan to get rich quick and pray that God will bless it. God will not answer selfish prayers for you to spend it on your pleasures.

If any of you lacks wisdom, let him ask of God, who
gives to all liberally and without reproach, and it will
be given to him. But let him ask in faith, with no
doubting, for he who doubts is like a wave of the sea
driven and tossed by the wind. – James 1:5-6

We must believe, and have faith in God that He will answer our prayers. We cannot doubt that He is a rewarder of those who seek and serve Him, worshiping and haveing the utmost respect for Him. When we ask of God, we must expect Him to answer our prayers liberally, generously, substantially, and freely. God takes joy in answering our prayers.

However, if we doubt Him or wonder if He will do it, then we blew it. Doubt is a prayer killer, a faith killer and has no positive role in the Kingdom of Light. A doubter is like a wave in the sea – believing this way one minute and then believing that way the next. A doubter is unstable in his thinking, and his unstable thinking will lead to unstable actions, and unstable actions will lead to certain destruction...

When we pray, we must believe God and pray according to His will and He will give us the answer we have been waiting for, according to His will. If you are not sure what His will is for your life, then read the Scriptures until it reveals itself in your spirit.

~

FAITH IS
by Paul Howard

[Faith is] — Faith enters in every part of life. Anything you want to accomplish, requires faith. Most people use faith every day without realizing it. You use your carnal faith when you turn on a switch, because you expect the lights to come on. Some want to achieve big things in life and are pursuing it with all they have. Others, once had dreams, but quit thinking about them; because their faith was weak.

Hebrews 11:1 KJV
Faith is the substance of things hoped for, the evidence of things not yet seen.

Your faith could've been built up by people encouraging you with positive re-enforcing words like *"you can accomplish anything in this world"* Or your faith was diminished because you heard all your life you were a loser. If you were of the latter, then I apologize for how those people that didn't have the love of God in them treated you.

Early in my Christian walk, the Pastor said something that changed my life. He was talking about how God took care of the birds; they didn't worry about their next meal or what they were going to wear *(See: Mt 6:25-34).* What really got me was: *"Are you not worth more than the birds?"* I was worth more than the birds. God would certainly take care of me. From that point on I've never worried about what I was going to eat, wear or even have a place to live; because, I knew God was concerned and He would take care of me.

When I was a little guy I was taught, The Bible was true; unquestionably *The Truth.* So, when I heard that sermon, it was true, and I had faith in it.

I studied my Bible and found many other passages that re-enforced my faith.

Philippians 4:19 KJV
My God shall supply all your need according to his riches in glory by Christ Jesus.

Deuteronomy 8:18b KJV
...remember the Lord Thy God for it is he that giveth

thee the power to get wealth...

Luke 11:9 KJV
And I say unto you, ASK, and it shall be given you;
seek and you shall find; Knock, and it shall be opened
unto you.

Mark 11:24 (para.)
Therefore, I tell you, whatsoever you ask in prayer,
believe that you received it, and it will be yours.

John 16:23-24 (para.)
In that day you will ask nothing of me. Truly, truly, I
say unto you, whatsoever you ask of the Father in my
name He will give it to you.

Matthew 21:22 ESV
And whatever you ask in prayer, you will receive, If
you have FAITH.

Faith is the key to having anything. *(cf. Jo 14:13, 15:16-17;*
1 Jo 3:22, 5:14-15) And the list goes on and on. You have
to have faith or these mean nothing to you.

You can be successful. You can be wealthy. You can be
healthy, you can have it all, if you only believe. Jesus said
you could lay hands on the sick and they shall recover
(See: Mk 16:17-18), but, that's a different chapter.

God wants to take care of you. It was not His intention for

you to be poor. According to *John 10:10*, the devil comes to do what? Steal, kill, and destroy. Jesus came that we could do what? Have life and have it more ABUNDANTLY.

He didn't intend for you to beg for food. He wants to take care of you, just like He takes care of the birds. Believe— have faith.

PRAYER OF INTERCESSION
by Jim Andrews

I was getting ready to leave for an appointment, when the Holy Spirit said to 'stop and pray.' I didn't know what I was praying for, so I prayed in the Spirit until release came. *(cf. Ro 8:26-27)* Then left for my appointment.

The next day, I received a call, telling me my brother-in-law had been attacked by a Texas Longhorn cow on his ranch. The cow picked him up and threw him in the air and he landed on his head, shoulder and arm. A man working near-by, saw what had happened and called an ambulance. He was life-flighted to the nearest hospital; the x-rays showed a broken neck, fractured spine, broken arm and hand. The hospital was not equipped to handle his type of injuries, so he was transferred to another hospital to see a specialist.

I found out it happened at the exact time I was quickened

to pray. The next day my brother-in-law was taken to surgery; the family was prepared by the doctor for the worst. The doctor came out of surgery weeping, stating that he did not understand what happened, the surgery was done in the O. R. (operating room), but—the healing took place up there (as he pointed to Heaven).

The doctor explained that this type of injury should have left him paralyzed as a quadraplegic; pointing out it was the same type of break a well known actor had been left paralyzed from.

He had two screws put in his neck and a cast on his arm. The third day he was home eating a steak. A miracle had taken place, because of obedience to stop and pray at the very moment the Holy Spirit spoke.

THE IMPORTANCE OF PATIENCE
IN POSSESSING YOUR 'PROMISED LAND'
by Bruce A. Higgins

Another very important truth the Lord taught me concerning my finances during this trial was—patience. The Lord reminded me that I didn't get into debt overnight, and that I wasn't going to get out of it overnight. Once again, the principle applies: that seed planted, must grow to maturity before it can be harvested.

I don't believe God ever leads us directly into trouble *(cf. Jo 8:12).* But I do believe that once we're in trouble, He will allow us to learn something from it. I learned a lot during this time of financial struggle, but the main thing I learned was patience.

One day I was impressed by the Lord to read about Joshua in the Old Testament. When Joshua took over the leadership of Isreal after Moses died, God commanded him to take the Israelites into the Promised Land to destroy the inhabitants and *possess the land (See. Jos 1:2-6).*

The Lord showed me that the inhabitants of Canaan could be likened to my bills, and those bills were invading my *"promised land"* of *prosperity.* He also showed me that just as Joshua took one city at a time, I too, would overcome one bill or loan at a time.

You see, the devil tries to get us to focus on all the adverse circumstances surrounding us, instead of patiently dealing with one problem at a time by faith. He wants us to feel overwhelmed by everything coming against us, so we'll give up and go down in defeat.

That's what Peter did when he got out of that boat and started to walk on the water. Everything was fine until he started to look at the circumstances—the wind and the waves; instead of Jesus *(See: Mt 14:29-30).*

The same is true with us. As long as we focus on the problem instead of on God's answer, we will always sink in defeat.

~

THE ANCHOR OF HOPE
by Pam Tattershall

The English word *"anchor"* comes from the Latin word *ancora*. Anchors symbolized hope in the Greek secular world. The Greek word for hope, agkura, is used as a vivid picture that keeps one steadfast in the midst of waves of doubt or stormy trials.

For the Christian, the writer of the book of Hebrews uses the Anchor as a vivid comparison of hope and stability, in the storms of life and death. In *Hebrews 6:18 & 19*, the Christian believer is clearly told, *"that by two immutable things, in which it is impossible for God to lie, we might have strong consolation, who have fled for refuge to lay hold of the hope set before us. This hope we have as an anchor of the soul, both sure and steadfast, and which enters the Presence behind the veil."* Our hope, as described by the author, is being held in place behind the veil by an anchor; consequently, this helps us to visualize what happens, when the Christian puts her or his hope and trust, into a Savior, Whose *presence* is behind the veil.

Behind the veil is the unseen, eternal reality of the heavenly world, while *the Anchor of Hope* has unique properties. It is *"both sure and steadfast."* Our hope is sure; it is not composed of doubt; its mooring cable will not break in the severe storm; no stress or strain upon it, and no resisting force will pull hope from its anchorage. Our hope is steadfast; unwavering in purpose, constant and firmly fixed amidst the turmoil's of life. The anchor is out of sight, but it holds, and that is what matters.

Since our hope is the anchor, we know that our hope is secured in God's very *presence* behind the veil, where Christ ever lives to make intercession for the Saints, according to the will of God.

"Wherefore also he is able to save to the uttermost them that draw near unto God through him, seeing He ever liveth to make intercession for them"
– Hebrews 7:25 KJV

The Apostle Paul drew near to God and prayed, when he experienced a tumultuous time during a sea voyage. The dark wind blew furiously, while the waves lapped over the boat, and eventually, the boat sank; however, Paul and all those who were on it were saved. The Anchor of Hope will save all those who put their trust in Him. These are truths from Paul's experience in *Acts 27*.

- Storms do come.
- Circumstances say all is lost.
- God's Word gives hope and direction in difficult times.

• What an anchor is to a vessel in its tossings, so hope is to us in our times of trial, difficulty, and stress.

Dear reader, the anchor was an ancient Christian symbol for safety, security, and hope. If you fear, if you doubt, place all of your trust in Christ: the "Anchor" who holds forever. Put your faith in the Blessed Hope. Jesus will hold you steadfast and secure.

~

TRUST AND REST IN HIM
by Michael Nokes

"Dedicated to Jacob Ray and Michael Noah Nokes"

Trusting in God is difficult when nothing is being seen. Beloved, build yourselves up in your *most holy faith*. SEEK HIM and you will find Him. This sounds like a promise from God our Father to us. He is saying He will *reveal His glory* to you if you obey Him diligently.

Diligence should never be confused with perfectness. We aren't perfect until He makes us perfect. God's definition of perfect is the seal of righteousness that is given by Him and determined more by our hearts than anything else.

God's things are always first. He works from the inside toward the outward man, not in reverse. This is why someone can be righteous, as deemed by God, yet their flesh still needs to be mortified or kept under control daily. It is important for us to *trust* Him and to *lean on* His understanding, not this world's tainted and distorted, trusting self or leaning to *the flesh*. The Word warns us that the heart of the flesh is deceitful. So let's believe God. We can trust Him! So if He has begun a work in someone and He deems them righteous during their walk, (while yet imperfect) we can rest in Him and trust Him that He will be *faithful* to complete the work in them. I mean hey, which one of us can discern the heart of someone to the depth of dividing asunder? Not me, I have tried and I have failed. Yet all this has worked for my good! This is why we see Him doing Perfect things through people that our flesh tries to judge as imperfect or ungodly.

Let us not call unclean what He has cleansed. And whatever you do, do not Judge the Heart of someone. Be led by the Spirit and Resist the Flesh.

~

HE ANSWERED MY PRAYER
by Nita G. Jones

I told the publisher of this book, my son Aaron, that I wanted to mention his name in this article. He said no at first but I talked him into it. The reason I wanted to mention his name and also my other son, Robert, is to say how proud and humble I am to have two sons God called to the ministry. Their Dad, Buck, felt the same way.

But when their Dad died suddenly, I was so afraid they would quit preaching. All the time the emergency paramedics were working with their Dad, I was praying that if he died, God would please help them to keep their faith, and not quit. He answered my prayer for both me and them. In that, because they stayed strong, I was also able to function.

But then, I began to lose my faith and kept asking God why this happened. Buck and I had been married for 39 years—I just couldn't understand. I couldn't read the Bible and I was really having a hard time. Yet, I still felt God's presence and love around me.

So, because of God's great love and my boy's faith, I eventually quit blaming God. He restored me, and both Aaron and Robert are still preaching The Gospel; not only that but also, I see their lives, and know they live what they preach.

God is so faithful. I thank and praise God for his love and mercy every day.

~

GOD'S WORD RESTORES
by Ed Marr
The following exerpt was taken from "FREEDOM V"
▪ Used by Permission.

Whereas, the worldly psychologist will try to figure out the motivating factors of his dysfunctional patient, based upon the imperfect model of basic human character or nature; God's Word regenerates and restores man's soul according to the perfect pattern of Christ! (*cf. 1 Co 11:1; 1 Pe 2:21*)

> *Hebrews 4:12 AMP*
> *"For the Word that God speaks is alive and full of power [making it active, operative, energizing and effective]; it is sharper than any two-edged sword, penetrating to the dividing line of the breath of life (soul) and [the immortal] spirit and of the joints and the marrow [of the deepest parts of our nature], exposing and sifting and analyzing and judging the very thoughts and purposes of the heart."*

~

TAKING NEW STEPS
by Rachel V. Jeffries

I was speaking by phone to a dear friend, whose husband moved to Heaven recently. They trusted each other and trusted in God. They prayed together regularly and highly respected each other. It has been a traumatic shock for her. She loves the Lord and is worshipping Him daily which keeps her at peace. New things are looming before her. I think most of us can identify. Men as well as women, must learn new things. Some men must learn to cook, iron, clean the house, etc. I suggest if you are going to cook, take a cooking class.

After my husband passed, I had never used a computer and had no desire to. When I was writing, someone else would enter them in the computer. The one doing the work, said to me, *"I think it is time for you to learn the computer."* I balked at that. She said, *"You are making too many changes which is making it hard for me to do the work."* I said, *"I heard of people crashing computers and I don't want to ever do that."* She said, *"You cannot crash a computer."* She joked later and said, *"I have changed my mind about that."* One morning an older lady was on the news program in Tulsa, Oklahoma. She announced a class for seniors who wanted to learn the computer. I registered and attended. It was like sending me off on a rocket ship.

Another challenge I faced, was a lack of direction. Today I have learned to follow signs; North, South, East and West. I have driven thousands of miles without fear and seldom get lost.

UNCTION TO FUNCTION

God gives us the unction to function. I want to say, *"My heart goes out to you if you are learning many things which your mate always did before."* Begin to say, *"I can do all things through Christ which strengthens me."* Rely on Him!

God has people everywhere who will help us, if we allow them to. Notice I said, *"God has them, not vultures of the enemy."*

I quote Kenneth Copeland, *"Your inner man is the source of the spiritual forces necessary for life on this planet."*

Proverbs 4:23 KJV
Keep thy heart with all diligence; for out of it are the issues of life.

The NLT says, *"Guard your heart above all else, for it determines the course of your life."*

Be blessed today!

PRAYER: Lord, I come to you in faith. I ask you to watch over me in everything. Help me not to be overwhelmed or panic when new opportunities come. I believe you have a new life for me. I accept it and walk in it, with the confidence of the Holy Spirit. I love you Lord. AMEN!

CONFESSION: I confess confidence in God. I have peace and will not panic. My beloved helps me beyond anything I have ever experienced. *My God meets all my needs according to His riches.* HALLELUJAH!

STANDING BY FAITH FOR HEALING
by Michael Nokes

On November 15th, 2012, I attended a Bible Study Group. There, was an older lady there that walked by the Spirit and it was obvious. That night, she testified about how God healed her diabetes. Somehow, I had been misled into believing that I understood positive confession. I don't know if it was the pride of my mind or direct or indirect deception from spiritual darkness. No matter the how, ultimately we know that Satan is the originator of *the lie* and that the truth, when revealed will set us free from bondage. When this lady gave her testimony, her words witnessed to my spirit. In one second, I was set free from years of deception.

This was her simple, yet powerful testimony: She told us that she had diabetes several years prior and that she had reached the point where her faith had risen up. She prayed and had already accepted her healing. However, one part of her story rang loud and clear to me. She said that she was in church one day and that the speaker knew of her fight against diabetes. He began to call up those with infirmities to the front for prayer. He then called her up, not by name but by her past infirmity, Diabetes. She said he called those up with diabetes several times even looking at her as he made the call. She said she almost got up to go, but sat back down. She said, *"No, I have been healed. I do not have diabetes."* She STOOD in the Spirit and stayed seated. She kept to her CONFESSION OF FAITH. She emphasized that from that day forward HER DIABETES WAS NO MORE. She received her healing at the moment she stayed seated.

A night or two later, I woke up with a dry scratchy patch in the back of my throat that kept coming and going over the next few nights. Each night the physical feeling would come upon my throat and each night I refused to negatively confess it. Instead on the last night, I remembered this ladies' CONFESSION OF FAITH, and made my own positive confession. I said, *"No, my throat is not getting sore, I was healed many years ago by the stripes that Jesus took for me. I have authority and will not use my authority to bring about sickness upon myself. I was healed and will not accept the serpent's lies. My throat is fine and no sickness is upon me or my children."* Rebuke the devil and he will flee and he DID. And I was healed instantly in that moment, with no reoccurrence.

~

THE LESSON OF THE HAMBURGER
by Ginny Bridges

"I wonder how many have missed their miracle by inspecting the vessel on the outside instead of expecting the gift that was on the inside?" Like E.F. Hutton, when Aaron Jones talks, people listen. So as I pondered his recent Facebook post, I knew God was planning to reveal something very special. He spoke *2 Corinthians 4:7 (KJV)* to me. *"We have this treasure in earthen vessels, that the excellency of the power may be of God, and not of us."* The Berean Study Bible puts it this way, *"Now we have this treasure in jars of clay to show that this surpassing great power is from God and not from us."*

What came to mind was a large patty made from a half

pound of USDA prime Angus, courtesy of a grass fed, sweet, docile cow free of additives, hormones, or chemicals.

Imagine it flame-grilled to perfection, juicy with the ideal tinge of pink in the center. The aroma is mouth-watering.

While cooking you to keep an eye on the process, anticipating its majestic deliciousness. Its nutritional value is off the charts—full of protein, vitamin B6, niacin, phosphorous, iron, vitamin B12, zinc, and a little calcium thrown in for good measure.

Imagine the perfectly prepared, top-of-the-line piece of beef then being removed from the grill and being placed on dry, stale, week-old white bread. Ugh! Your appetite has just taken a dive. That hamburger has become ugly to the eye, and unappealing to your taste buds, and you push it away.

Now use your imagination to see that same patty on a fresh ciabatta bun. See it accompanied by fresh tomatoes, lettuce, pickles or onion, the best mayo—exactly what you ordered. Ah, now your appetite has returned, and your salivary glands are in overdrive.

Yet no matter the packaging, the nutritional value is unchanged. It's still laden with vitamins and minerals. It's still prime sirloin. There's no difference in the meat. It isn't affected at all by the presentation.

And so it is sometimes with soul or spirit food from God.

Occasionally His Word, will be presented to us via a well-dressed, highly educated, perfectly coifed and manicured Sister Pearly Teeth or Brother Samuel Suave. We stand in the ministry line, no matter how long it takes, to receive a precious treasure from God, a word of encouragement, a blessing, a prayer.

Then again, He just might send His gift wrapped in an unkempt, illiterate, clumsy, or broken vessel. Then we are offended at the lack of finesse, and we reject the message because the messenger doesn't quite fit the ideal mold.

We need to remember that god is God all by Himself, He doesn't need our help to be God. He doesn't require our input, our opinions, or our expectations in order to do what He deems best. He gets to decide how to create and give gifts to His children. He develops the courier, and selects the time and place for delivery.

Rev. Keith Moore, Faith Life Church in Branson, MO., says *"God gave gifts to men. And ministry gifts. It doesn't mean they're smarter than you. It wouldn't even neccessarily mean they are more spiritual than you. It wouldn't even neccessarily have meant they knew more Word than you. You might ask, "Well, then, why should I listen to them?" Because God chose them and gave them a place in your life, and what they have that you don't have is an anointing for that place. And God will give them things that will help you."*

So let's stop discarding the treasure, because the wrapping doesn't meet our standard. Our responsibility is to discern the gift and receive it fully, not critique the package. How about if we accept that God can use us, even us, to minister to someone in all our frailty, brokenness, issues, and failures? Make a commitment to humbly accept a treasure from Him without judging His emissary. Including the one in the mirror.

~

EPHESIANS 1:17 PROPHECY
by Daryl P Holloman
(Received [11/23/18] in Broken Arrow, Oklahoma)

[For I always pray to] the God of our Lord Jesus Christ, the Father of glory, that He may grant you a spirit of wisdom and revelation [of insight into mysteries and secrets] in the [deep and intimate] knowledge of Him, – Ephesians 1:17 Amplified Bible

There is a Well of Revelation just for you

From where the Holy Ghost can draw

And show you what to do

You must have an ear to hear

What the Spirit of God is saying

His Written Word will make it clear

Because His Word and Spirit agree

Study and Pray to obey

The end result will make you free

He will show you Mysteries

He will show you Secrets

To keep you from all miseries

Revealing who you are In Him

Revealing Who He is in you

Delivering you through thick and thin

He will bring you through the Fire

He will bring you through the Water

He will bring you through the Quagmire

Wisdom is yours for the receiving

Standing and Speaking His Word

From a Heart of Faith and Believing

He is your Wisdom you know

He will Guide and Direct your Way

So Go with the Holy Ghost and Flow

He will Reveal what you need to Know

Changing Your Life as You Go

To Help You Cause Others to Grow

So Rejoice and Be Exceedingly Glad

Rise Above Your Being Mad

Living a Life that is No Longer Sad

Your Destiny is Not in a Ditch

As You Walk in His Glory and Light

Your Life Now In Christ Jesus is Rich

IDENTIFIED WITH US
by Michael Hicks

Why did Jesus, the Son of God lay down His power to come to Earth as a man. Some will say, *"So we can receive salvation"* and that is right. Some will say, *"To teach us the ways of God"* and that is also right. These answers are true. But there is one I do not hear too much about, and that is: *He came to identify with us.* Jesus came from Heaven to Earth to live as a man, who listened to God and followed God's instructions. Remember, He only said what God said and did what He saw God do. So Jesus was a person made of flesh, just like us. He ate dinner like us, He drank water like us, He bathed like us, talked like us, walked like us, used the restroom like us and He was even tempted like us. I am almost positive that the devil sent women to Him to seduce Him, but to no avail. In fact, He was tempted in every way we are, but—He did not sin. He came down to experience personally, what we as the human race are plagued with.

Now Jesus set the example for us and it is the blueprint for ministry and life.

> For I have not spoken on My own authority; but the Father who sent Me gave Me a command, what I should say and what I should speak. – John 13:49 NKJV

Jesus did not come from Heaven to do His own thing. He did not come to lord over the people of the earth. He came by command from God the Father to speak what God speaks and do what God does. It was God who worked through Jesus to heal the sick, to raise the dead, to teach people about the Kingdom of God.

> Do you not believe that I am in the Father, and the Father in Me? The words I speak to you I do not speak on My own authority; but the Father who dwells in Me does the works. Believe Me that I am in the Father and the Father in Me, or else believe Me for the sake of the works themselves. – John 14:10-11 NKJV

When Jesus was baptized by John the Baptist, the Holy Spirit descended like a dove from Heaven and alighted upon Him. He did not do any miracles before the Spirit of God fell on Him. But after the Spirit of God came upon Him, He was equipped to do the miracles He became famous for. Jesus stayed in the framework of doing what the Father says and saying what the Father says. So everytime He preached the Word, lives changed.

∽

SPEAK BOLD TRUTH
by Aaron Jones

Never apologize, for what I despise.
Don't be apologetic, over what I reject.
It's not being cold, to be bold.
You're hot when you tell what's what.

Pay no attention to men's opinions,
or the devil's little minions.
You speak the bold truth,
My Word is your proof.

Never be fake'in
Compromised, or shaken.
Not diluted or stirred,
Just tell them My Word.

The enemy is playing for keeps,
So, birth some lambs, and feed my sheep.
Bring them to Heaven, eternity's at stake
The alternative's too hot and no goats will I take.

So get it in gear, they all need to hear,
Hell will be burning, and Jesus returning.

We're nearing that day, when the Master will say,
Welcome home my Friend, or sadly this is your end.

When time is no more, We'll settle up the score.
They'll open the book, God will take a look.
If you're saved, it's into Heaven, if not cast to Hell.
Jesus Christ is the way in, that's all I can tell.

CRY OUT FOR THE CRUMBS
by Brian Ohse

(Based on Matthew 15:22-28)

A woman comes to Jesus crying out for her daughter to be healed and delivered from a demon, [something very few churches talk about]. She recognizes this is no ordinary battle, but a spiritual one; so, she starts searching for this Jesus that she's heard so much about. And low and behold she runs right into Him.

As she is running toward Him, she crys out from the depth of her soul for her daughter's life to be restored. She doesn't care who sees her, what she looks like, or even what words she speaks. She's going with an expectation; *believing for a miracle.* She has already decided nothing will stop her. But what does she cry out? *"Have mercy on me Lord!"* She was saying, show me forgiveness, even when I don't deserve it. Show me true compassion. Then she says, *"Son of David,"* meaning You came from the promise given to Abraham, yes, you are a man, but much more than a man. For I have heard of the miracles and wonders you have done.

But Jesus does not respond, it looks like she came all this way for nothing. Then she hears His disciples asking Jesus to get rid of her, saying, *"send her away"*. Her heart is tearing apart. How many times do we feel The Lord has abandoned us, and isn't even listening? We cry out, but it seems His ears are deaf. Then she switches gears and starts worshiping Him; bowing down, asking for help. But still, Jesus does not respond favorably. For He says, *"It's not right to take the children's bread and cast it to dogs."*

At this point, she could have walked away defeated, but instead she pressed in with these words, *"Truth Lord, yet the dogs eat the crumbs which fall from their master's table."*

Why was this statement her miracle turn-around?

For the answer, lets look at the natural for a minute. If you give a dog table scraps, he recives it as a feast. So she was saying, the truths that other people have missed, or discarded—I receive as a feast from Your table. For I hear and see things that others do not. So ask The Father, through The Holy Spirit to show you the crumbs that are hidden in The Word, that others have missed.

"Cry out for the crumbs!"

~

THE SILENT YEARS OF JESUS
by Bobby Lampkin

According to Jewish History, by the time a male child was 10, they had to memorize the first five books of Moses. Also called the *Pentateuch*. It consisted of the following books; Genesis, Exodus, Leviticus, Numbers, and Deuteronomy. They had to quote all these books by memory. Then at the age of thirteen, they were responsible for obeying the laws they were taught. By the age of fifteen they were required to study the wisdom of Jewish sagas and other Jewish teachings. By the age of 20 they were ready for a career, often in the family business. Joseph was a carpenter, and this is the reason Jesus was a carpenter. Jesus was a carpenter until the age of 30. Thirty was the age according to Jewish history a man could become a rabbi in those days. Jesus was at the temple at the age of twelve, the scribes were astonished at what Jesus knew.

Luke 2:46-47 KJV
46 And it came to pass, that after three days they found him in the temple, sitting in the midst of the doctors, both hearing them, and asking them questions.
47 And all that heard him were astonished at his understanding and answers.

From the time of birth until the age of twelve, Jesus was taught by His Pastors. Joseph and Mary.

Twelve is the age of accountability, 12 also means a new government. From twelve to age thirty is 18 years of silence. Ten plus eight. Ten in scripture means a new dimension, eight means a new beginning.

What does that mean? A new beginning of a new dimension of God. This new dimension started, when Jesus was baptized by John the Baptist at the age of 30. What happened when Jesus was baptized? The Heavens were opened.

How many of you have ever been at a place that seemed like God, where did you go? I know in my personal life I have thought that many times. Sometimes God speaks in different ways then what we are accustomed to. Don't lose hope my friend, God has you right where He wants you.

Even Jesus Who was the Son of God, went through a time in His life that seemed like God had forgotten Him. From the time Jesus was 12 to the age of 30 was 18 years. Can you imagine God being silent for 18 years? We can't go three weeks without hearing from God, until we start to panic. Don't panic my friend, God has you right where you need to be.

Jesus did what He knew to do, until the appointed time came to be the redeemer for all mankind.

~

IT'S JUST A CHAIR
by Steve Farmer

True story:

Years ago, I woke up, and KNEW someone or something was in my room. Fear gripped me, and I sat up quickly.

My wife was asleep, and I heard no noise, but, panic swept over me as I looked at the foot of my bed: there stood a demon looking at me...

He never made a sound, but I could see his shape, and tremors of "fear" swept over me... I whispered Jesus over and over, I cried out *"Blood of Jesus!"* I closed my eyes and prayed that God would do something!!!!

After a few minutes of "eyes closed," heart racing minutes of sheer panic, as the light of morning began to gradually come into the room, I gathered my nerve to look again.....

It was just a chair, with my coat wrapped around it and my stocking hat on top of it.......

Fear may have you frozen and feeling helpless, trapped with no place to run, but open up your heart to the light of God's Word, And as the light comes in, you will finally see... It was ...JUST A CHAIR!!!

CHRIST FOLLOWERS
by Heather Wright

Christ followers are known by their love and by their fruit. That means we are choosing to spread love. You can either spread love or you can spread chaos. You can bring joy or you can bring sorrow. Christ didn't die for perfect people, he died for sinners. He died for me and you. He tells us to love one another as we love ourselves *(Gal 5:14).* That means, in order to fully be able to love others, we have to know—who we are in Christ.

Our identity should be in Christ. It shouldn't be in other people, but in Christ alone. We should be clothed in righteousness *(Job 29:14).* While we are called to love, we are also called to stand up for what is right *(Gal 5:1).* In all ways, acknowledge him and He will make your paths straight *(Prov 3:6).*

This hits home for me. From certain people in my past, I was told that I was not good enough and that I was always the problem. I had to learn on my own, with Jesus leading me, how to fully love myself and see myself the way He sees me. You are a new creation in Christ Jesus.

"Therefore, if anyone is in Christ, the new creation has come: The old has gone, the new is here."
— 2 Corinthians 5:7

Don't ever let someone bring you down to a place where you don't want to be. Rise up with boldness and know that you are the head and not the tail! You are above and not beneath!

~

GET KNOWLEDGE, UNDERSTANDING, AND WISDOM
by Jan Collins

Young people have their own language, vernacular and perceptions of Christians and church in general, than people born in the Twentieth Century.

People of all ages, not just the young, may not know how to get over things.

GET OVER IT!

An older and perhaps wiser Christian individual could help them "get over it." There are basic biblical steps to moving forward from past issues or baggage. Could you be instrumental in helping their spiritual growth by accepting a person the same way God accepted you? *Getting* is a key word.

Get knowledge, understanding, and wisdom: Knowledge is empowering. The more one understands God's Word, the more one understands their life's purpose. Knowledge and understanding are not enough. People need to use wisdom on how to apply the knowledge, to truly achieve success in life. God can help change one's thought processes if their desire is strong enough. Making wise decisions, can bring freedom and restoration.

GET OVER YOURSELF!

Compassion toward others is mercy, but when it's turned inward, mercy becomes self-pity. In the midst of self-pity, is where depression and other negative emotions dwell. Could you be instrumental in showing young people how to reaching out to others and giving of oneself? Can you help a person to be more grateful of who they are and what they have—and what they have actually accomplished so far in life? Sincerely caring and reaching out to others, can help one forget about their own problems and turn the "self-pity" around into "mercy" for others. It can be a productive journey to wellness of one's soul and help set a person free and draw them into the Kingdom of God.

By praying, studying and seeking God's direction, He can show you to whom you are to minister, how to relate and what to say.

For extended reading: *Psalm 18:28, 49:3; Philippians 3:13*

~

DIVISION, FEAR, AND CONFUSION
by Michael Nokes

I am so tired of the devil. Every time something good is getting ready to begin, he swoops in. He comes to steal, kill, and destroy. He is the author of confusion. He divides, divides, divides; and you notice, he never divides based on Christian or non-Christian. No, instead he uses *Republican v Democrat* to divide Christians. He uses *beautiful v plain* to divide Christians. He uses *fit v fat* to divide Christians. He uses *rich v poor* to divide Christians. He even uses *women v men* to divide Christians! That devil uses *fear* and *pride* in every one of these situations to bring about division in the "body of Christ." Yes, this is the body that's supposed to be tightly knit and fitted together. And the worst part is: most of our churches allow these divisions based on fears they entertain.

Look at this world and see why! So, *resist the devil and he will flee!*

~

TAKE TIME TO WRITE
by Molly Sue Allday

I write for many reasons. I want to tell you about them. Maybe it will encourage you and others to write.

One reason I write is to record the things I hear the Lord say to me, so I can pray over them and incorporate them into my vision and goals. I also write to express thoughts that are going on in me, which helps me clarify those thoughts and discern what God is saying to me and what I need to do, and decisions I need to make. Writing also helps one deal with negative emotions or any emotions going on inside. As one writes, it can help diffuse emotions and put them in their proper place. David did this when he was writing psalms. He would start off rehearsing all the negative things that were happening to him, and then he would turn it around into a prayer to God, praising God and remembering all the things He had done for him before.

I write music and add lyrics as an expression of love to the Lord and as a creation He puts in my heart to bless Him and others. I know it will bless others and bring them healing and deliverance because I am worshipping. He dwells in our praise, so my praise will bring others into His presence. I often write as I am sitting at the piano worshipping, or even while I am driving in the car. He will put a melody in my mind and I will start singing it. Or He will put a phrase with a tune in my spirit that I just start singing out, sometimes in a spontaneous ministry setting.

I write as an expression of what God has done for me and add that He can do it for others.

I know that many times when I write, it is just for me and the Lord, but I also believe that someday people who come after me may read my journals and it may minister to them. When I write songs of worship, many times it is from me to the Lord. But I record many of them, because I know they may turn into longer songs that can be used to help others as well to enter into worship.

Writing is an expression of the Holy Spirit working within me. I believe it would benefit every believer to write. I believe it is also important to teach children to write, to express what is in their hearts, and to help them process their thoughts and feelings. Our words are creative and powerful, as we are all created in His image. He spoke, and it was so. In the same way, when we speak, or write, it is a creative force that can bring life to the world around us. I believe it blesses the Father, because we are speaking what He has given us to speak.

~

BEFITTING A QUEEN
by Marcella O'Banion Burnes

Jewelry befitting a queen
A most unusual thing

Not broken baubles of bright glass
But precious things that will last

Cost alone
Paid for by an ethereal throne

Willing participants, believers they say

Who'll wear these jewels on a wedding day

When the Bride of Christ shall rise
Before all eyes into the skies

Adorned with things not of this world
But of priceless cost
Far greater than rubies or pearls

Opening a box, a treasure trove,
We, like children should pilfer in droves

Right before our very eyes
Loves been given in ample supplies

Peace like a river does flow
Out of our belly's it comes from that trove

Joy in abundance, No cares
The world will see what we wear

Healing, leaves from the tree of life
All partakers of this will know what it's like

Prayer?
Boots on the ground
A mighty war cry should resound

Singing out a joyful noise
Preparing praise should be always

A prophet's word prepares the troops
Can sometimes cause to holler and whoop

Precious precious precious are these
Jewelry draped on a bride to be

~

GOD DOESN'T CONDEMN US
FOR OUR MISTAKES
by Bruce A. Higgins

Now, before you start asking me, *"Why did you ever let yourself get into that situation?"* Remember, we have all done things in life we shouldn't have.

When someone has gotten himself in a difficult situation for whatever reason, the last thing he needs is condemnation. For instance, one time I was pulling a trailer full of furniture behind my pickup, and i blew out a tire. I pulled over to the side of the road, and a man stopped to help me.

This man was a real blessing to me in helping me put another tire on the vehicle. However, the whole time he was helping me, he preached a sermon of condemnation to me about how stupid I was for overloading the trailer. I knew I had made a mistake in packing the load, but I didn't need this man hammering that point home on the side of the interstate with hundreds of semi-trucks flying by us at top speed!

According to *Romans 8:1*, God doesn't put condemnation on His children. We have all made mistakes, so instead of judging one another *(cf. Mt 7:1)*, let's look into God's Word for answers to help us out of our problems.

One more, very important point along this line is this: God isn't the one bringing these problems to test you or make you strong. I dislike that type of thinking.

God loves you, and you are His child. The God of Heaven is your very own Father, and He will help you if you ask Him and believe His Word. He is the God who promises you, *"Call unto me, and I will answer thee, and shew thee great and mighty things, which thou knowest not"* (Je 33:3).

I remember driving around one night pondering a teaching I had recently heard on a Christian television program. The minister on this program had taught about how God tries us and puts us through the fire. Then a few days later, I heard another very popular minister teach along the same lines, relating the ways God had tested him and the church he pastors. According to both of these well-known ministers, God had put the pressure on them for one reason or another.

As I drove, I asked God what His perspective was regarding what those two ministers had taught. I knew that according to *James 1:13*, God doesn't test with evil. But many preachers sidestep this Scripture by reasoning, *"Yes, but God is doing this for our good."*

As I asked the Lord for a clear answer to this age-old teaching that God puts us through the fire, He spoke these Words so clearly to my heart: *"When I test My children, it's from the inside out (meaning from the heart or spirit of man outward). When the devil tests My children, it's from the outside in."*

But when God leads you to do something, such as to give a special offering, He doesn't bombard your mind with such thoughts as, *"If you don't do this, you're going to Hell."* No, He just quietly speaks to your heart to do it. If you obey, you have passed God's test.

> *Proverbs 17:3 KJV*
> *The fining pot is for silver, and the furnace for gold: but the LORD trieth the hearts.*

HAVE YOU READ YOUR BIBLE TODAY?
by Aaron Jones

Over and over again, I have posted this question on Facebook and Twitter: *"Have you read your Bible today?"*

Why, do I ask? Because I believe it is one of, if not the most important thing a person can choose to do with their time.

I've often said, *"The #1 SIN on Earth is: people are not reading and studying The Bible. If they were, things would be different; if the sinner read The Bible, they would get saved, and if the saints read The Bible, they would know how to act."*

Have you read it? Have you read The Bible? It's God's Word you know, He used authors from all walks of life over hundreds of years to pen down His will for you and I. Shouldn't we read it? It's the wisdom of an eternal Creator, wrapped in love and sent to His creation. Shouldn't we read it? It tells the end (the future) from the beginning (beforehand) accurately. Shouldn't we read it? It tells about the end of all things. Shouldn't we read it? Historians have tried to invalidate it, while scientists have tried to disprove it. Evil men have burned it and tried to destroy it, governments have confiscated and tried to outlaw it. Shouldn't we read it? Men have died to keep it, others have died to get it, while still others (missionaries) have died to give it away. Shouldn't we read it?

Someone once said the *acronym* for "Basic Instructions Before Leaving Earth" is the word *'BIBLE.'* Think about that!

John 1:1-4 KJV
1 In the beginning was THE WORD, and THE WORD was with God, and <u>THE WORD was God</u>.
2 The same was in the beginning with God.
3 <u>All things were made by him; and without him was not any thing made that was made.</u>
4 In him was life; and the life was the light of men.

Hebrews 11:3 KJV
Through faith we understand that the worlds were framed by THE WORD OF GOD, so that things which are seen were not made of things which do appear.

Romans 10:17 KJV
So then faith [cometh] by hearing, and hearing by THE

WORD OF GOD.

Hebrews 1:3a KJV
Who being the brightness of [his] glory, and the express
image of his person, and upholding all things by THE
WORD of his power...

"It's the B - I - B - L - E,

Yes, that's the Book for me,

I stand alone on The Word of God,

The B - I - B - L - E!"

I have to ask once again, *"Have you read your Bible today?"*

ONE IN GOD
by Michael Hicks

When we repented of our sins and accepted Jesus as our
Lord and Savior, the Holy Spirit came upon us. I did not
see anything fall upon me, but I felt the weight of my
many, many sins come off me. I felt as light as a feather
and was extremely relieved. I was born again. I was no
longer blind and ignorant to the Word of God, because
the Holy Ghost gave me clarity and I began understanding the Scriptures. I was no longer a slave to sin, because
the nature of God was now in me.

Most assuredly, I say to you, he who believes in Me,

the works that I do he will do also; and greater works than these he will do, because I go to My Father.
— John 14:12 NKJV

In order for us to do this, we must let ourselves go and plug into The Holy Spirit. The Holy Spirit that dwelled in Jesus is the same Holy Spirit that dwells in believers of the gospel. When we were baptized, God changed our sin nature and replaced it with His. *Behold, old things, (our sin nature), have passed away and all things have become new.* We are no longer kids of the devil but children of the *true* and *living* God.

When Jesus was conducting His earthly ministry, He could only be at one place at a time. Now if God wanted, He could have translated Jesus as He did with Philip in *Acts 8*, but He did not. Even though He did all those wonderful miracles – He could only be at one place at a time.

Nevertheless, I tell you the truth. It is to your advantage that I go away; for if I do not go away, the Helper will not come to you; but if I depart, I will send Him to you. – John 16:7 NKJV

The ministry of Jesus was as a man filled with the Spirit of God. When Jesus left the earth to go back to God, He sent the Holy Spirit to the believers on the earth. The Holy Spirit is not limited as Jesus was. The Holy Spirit is a spirit without boundaries, whereas Jesus had boundaries, because He was man in a skin suit. The Holy Spirit can be all over the world at the same time. So these are the greater works Jesus told us about, every believer can do what Jesus did. However, instead of only eleven born again disciples, there are millions of born again believers around the world.

The most wonderful benefit to being a born again believer is: we are now *one in God, one in the Son,* and *one in the Holy Spirit.* God is one with us, God the Son is one with us and God the Holy Spirit is one with us.

> *I do not pray for these alone, (the eleven disciples), but for those who will believe in Me through their word; that they all may be One, as You Father are in Me, and I in You; that they also may be one in Us, that the world may believe that You sent Me.*
> *– John 17:20-22 NKJV*

It is a privilege to be one in God, as God is one with you. To be one in Christ, as Christ is one with you. To be one in the Holy Spirit, as the Holy Spirit is one with us. I believe that this is one of the greatest gifts in the world, given by the true and living God. We need to wrap our minds in these Scriptures, and meditate on them day and night until they become our life. Then we will eventually fulfill the Scriptures as Jesus intends for us to do.

I WIN
by Paul Howard

I long to hear His Words.
They comfort me day and night
I know that He is with me
I know I win the fight.

"I will never leave or forsake you,"
That's what He said to me.
"I will always be right with you
Especially on your knees."

I hear His Word in my heart
It may seem strange to thee
He feeds the many sparrows
I know, He will feed me.

One day I will join Him
In that land beyond the sky
I hope that you'll come with me
If Him you will not deny

Yes, His Words are a comfort
They comfort me day and night
I can feel Him with me
And I know I win the Fight

~

WRINKLED HANDS
by Bill Steinmetz

My hands are wrinkled, worn,
tattered, and torn.
As I've grown old, I've become more bold
to walk in the dark and the cold.

I do what I can to help every man who asks me to
Sometimes I just can't
and they can just rant I just can't.
My life has been changed by a man who can change me.
He's flipped and flopped and so rearranged me.

Some laugh and scoff
and behind my back they talk and mock.
I really don't mind,
my friend just says be kind,
if you've a mind to.

If you don't know what I'm saying,
know this I'll be praying.
If you gain the whole world and all of its gold,
it won't mean a thing when you get too old,
you'll be out in the COLD.

My hands are wrinkled and tattered,
not that it mattered.

1984 TO 2013
by Len Blanchard

The year was 1984. We, from the Lyons FWB Church, were having an outdoor event at a member's home. I became distracted as I felt the Lord was dealing with me. I walked off to be alone. I began to see many things in my mind that I did not fully comprehend at the time. Feeding the needy, prisoners set free coming to our church, food bank, clothing for the needy, many people coming and going, a church school, friendly atheists sitting and speaking freely with me and others, a "Think Tank,"** and a minister's retirement center were things whirling around in my mind.

It wasn't long before some of my men found me. Our church had "taken off" spiritually and numerically. I shared with them all that God was saying to me. I still do not know if that was a good decision or bad for it made them believe that God was going to do all that right there in their midst. To be honest, I thought that as well. But that is not how it all worked out.

Years passed and I saw some things accomplished at one place and some things accomplished at another. Yet, the vision was never fully satisfied in my spirit. Was I to never be satisfied with what I was convinced the Lord put into my spirit? I wondered that over and over. But then......

2013 came and I moved to Sapulpa, Oklahoma. When I saw the spot where the church sat, there was an overwhelming move in me that said, *"Here, here is where it will be finished."* In five short years the Lord has given us a Preschool, an Academy, Cans for Crossroads food ministry, a Women's Sober Living facility, support of a Men's Sober Living Facility, prisoners who have been set free attending our church in good numbers, and those still praying for a "Think Tank" and Minister's Retirement Center. We thought we may have had the Center about a year and half ago, but wasn't meant to be at the time.

Some of you who are reading this may feel God isn't going to finish in you what you knew to be Him. Let me tell you, *"God is a Finisher, not just a "Dreamer."* I was 32 when the vision came. I am 66 today and wonderfully happy and blessed. Hold on! Trust Him! He will take you to your journey's end. *"Philippians 1:6"*

**Think Tank – a building built in circular fashion with no corners, only seating and massive bookshelves. A place to entertain "thinkers," atheists, non-believers, etc. to freely sit without judgement to share their beliefs and concerns to discuss life and what each believes it holds.

HE IS OUR ROCK
by Aaron Jones

When troubles come,
And we all know they will.
Don't you fear or run,
Instead, dare to stand still.

No matter how bad the story,
No matter how hard,
Don't dare start to worry,
Keep your eyes fixed on God.

With your back to the wall,
Like your racing the clock.
He won't let you fall,
Christ alone is your Rock.

When at a loss what to do,
God's timing seems late,
Know He is there for you,
Just remain stedfast in faith.

The answer is already given,
The works all complete,
Keep expecting the blessing,
And the victory you'll see.

Stand your ground in Jesus' Name,

This is not religious idle talk!
By faith we've already overcame
In Christ Jesus—OUR ROCK!

TWO CROSSES: REFLECTIONS ON A TWITTER CONVERSATION
by Adrienne Gottlieb

While reading my Twitter time line, I came across this tweet:

"If you don't have Jesus on your Cross in your Church, Do U have the true Presence of Jesus in Communion, in the teachings? Or: Empty Cross?"

But wait, I thought: He is risen, no longer on the cross.

Of course, Jesus died on the cross for me, taking away my sins; dying in my place. Without this sacrifice, I wouldn't be forgiven and would remain in a state of sin expecting to meet the devil upon my demise. But that's not the case, thank God. Jesus did do that remarkable work on the Cross; but His work did not end there. If it did, I and many others would be worshipping a dead person. How foolish would that be?

The fact is: after defeating the devil, and releasing the captives by taking the keys of Death and Hades—Jesus rose from the dead. The Scripture states that my life is hidden in Christ life *(See: Col 3:3)*. You see I died with Christ and

I also rose with Him. His resurrection gives me the ability to lead a victorious life while I am still here on earth. That's how I became a new creation *(cf. 2 Co 5:17)*.

As a new person in Him, I have power over the enemy (the devil) and power to conquer the trials and tribulations of life. I get to serve a risen, alive God. *(cf. Heb 7:25* and *Eph 1:20)*. While I remember what Christ did for me on the Cross, I commune with my Risen Savior. I can't leave Him on that Cross. I think so many Christians miss the joy of Christianity because they fail to see the victory of His Ascension on a daily basis. Jesus is making intercession for me right now to Father God. He is alive. When I commune with Him and pray, I am speaking to someone who is no longer on that Cross, but one who is alive and wants to have fellowship with me. How glorious is that?

While it is good to remember Christ did die for us, it is also and always important to remember that He is alive in us, not some far off place in the sweet by and by. The same Spirit who raised Christ from the dead dwells in me *(See: Ro 8:11)* fellowships or communes with me and empowers me to live a victorious life in Him. It doesn't get any better than that. So, when I commune with Christ as His child, acknowledging that yes, He went to the cross for me, but at the same time realizing where He is seated now, I then can commune with that cross being empty!

He is now risen and He lives in me. I pray that you can say the same.

~

THE STRUGGLE
AND THE POINT OF COMMITMENT
by Michael Nokes

Something peculiar has happened to me. I see struggle completely different than I once did.

I can remember [as a child] that I wanted to be a Christian so that I could avoid worldly *hardships* and *struggles*. I had seen suffering, but I didn't want to suffer; therefore, I avoided it, and even ran from it at times. Then later in life when it hit me, it would paralyze me; I didn't understand it.

Do not get me wrong, it is natural to *not* desire hardship and struggle. But now, I have come to more fully rest in and understand God's great love for all His creation. I now accept His leadings, and why as His *peculiar people*, that *'peculiar'* tends to get sprinkled in as salt and light. But there is a price to pay, it's a sacrifice; some are willing, some are not. Jesus said *there is no greater love than to lay down your life for a friend.* And through it, always remember: *His yoke is easy and His burden is light.*

Nothing evil moves me anymore; I am only moved by God and interested in His habitations. *Psalm 91:7-10,* holds deeper meaning to me than ever before. And reading through *the Book of Job* many times, opened my eyes to understanding God's ways.

I see an immensely powerful and wise God. I see a God of immeasurable understanding. I see a God of Love. I see a God Who is so confident in the outcome, that He can let you fail and patiently await your return.

God is immovable, He is unchangeable; henceforth, this life is not about Him. This *life is a gift* to us, it's about us— it's about changing us; because He loves us! It is about *new* hearts. It is about *changing* desires. It is about *creating* change in us, and for us; for the better. It's about beauty springing from darkness. As Job said it is wondrous.

Job's *point of commitment* is described, in *Job 42:5-6, 10 (KJV). Verse 5, I have heard of thee by the hearing of the ear: BUT NOW MINE EYE SEETH THEE. Verse 6, Wherefore I abhor myself, and repent in dust and ashes.* And then *verse 10, And the Lord turned the captivity of Job, WHEN HE PRAYED FOR HIS FRIENDS.* [Catch the revelation of this.]

What has God done for you at your point of commitment? Or, did you fail the test(s) of commitment? Not that God tested you necessarily, but more than likely you have had opportunities of testing set before you.

∼

YOU CAN'T HEAR WHAT
YOU'RE NOT LISTENING FOR
by Paul Thomas Adams

While driving local for a large trucking company, I would occasionally pass within 200 yards of my home situated in a small housing community just off the highway here in northeast Oklahoma. I had spoken to my wife minutes earlier and asked what her and the kids were doing, age 5/9. She said they were in the pool in the back yard. I did not tell her I was going to be driving by on the highway in 10 minutes or less. As I approached the turnoff from 69 Hwy. into our development, I laid into the air horn on the tractor, this thing is obnoxious loud and can be heard a mile away. Upon arriving home, I asked my wife if her or the kids heard me honking at them, and she said no. I shared with her that I had honked the air horn three times, so they could hear me. She said neither her or the kids heard the horn. My daughter asked if I was driving by tomorrow and I told her probably not. I told my wife Robin to make sure they were swimming at the same time tomorrow and I would honk from the highway as I drove by, but don't tell the kids. The next afternoon I called on her cell phone, and said, don't tell them it's me on the phone.

I said to let them keep playing and splashing and I'll honk here in about one minute, so stay on the phone, so I can hear their reactions if any. I laid into the air horns with three quick and one long blast and they immediately began screaming, it's daddy' it's daddy, we hear you daddy, we love you: What time are you coming home? I heard my daughter, Alicia say to her mother, that's really loud mom, how come we didn't hear him yesterday? She said yesterday you were not *expecting* or *listening* for your father, but today you were!

People are always asking me, Pastor Paul: Does God really talk to you? You say in your sermons, that God told you this or that. My response is always the same, if you're not hearing from Him, it's probably because you're not expecting Him to talk, or not listening for Him. Anticipate and listen for Him, and you will hear His Voice. *[Honk, honk!]*

PEACE
by Paul Howard

Once like a Bird
Is how I felt
Going to and fro
No rest for self

From place to place
I wondered blind
Longing for peace
I could not find

Then one day
One Glorious day
I found a Place
The Place to stay

No more to labor
Peace I found
In the Arms of My savior
His arms wrapped around

Now I am grounded
No wondering about
I found Jesus
In Him there's no doubt

DISAPPOINTMENTS
by Barbara J. White

Sometimes in life we experience disappointments. A disappointment can be either a stumbling block or a stepping stone; it all depends on how we deal with it.

We must never blame God, He is never the source of our disappointments. To fail to achieve what we hope and believe for causes anxiety and even embarrassment.

We must turn the spotlight on ourselves, our decisions and actions. How did this happen? Condemnation will

The GOD of the MOUNTAIN II

soon rear its ugly head but we know God never condemns
us. So, what do we do?

The God-kind of faith, is based on what God has said and
provided for us in His Word. When God's Word is abiding
in us, and we are abiding in Him, we can ask what we will
and it will be done *(See: John 15:7).* John tells us to *have confidence in God, and if we ask anything according to His will,
He hears us and we know that if He hears us we have the peti-
tions that we desired of Him.* So: Where does the problem lie
when disappointments come? *(cf. 1 John 5:14-15)*

Gordon and I learned an important lesson many years
ago. We were young and had much more to learn in the
area of faith. Living in England at the time, we decided it
would be good to visit my parents in Canada. We booked
our plane tickets "in faith" and continued to thank God
for the financial provision. The day came for our depar-
ture and it passed without the money for the tickets!
Where did we go wrong?

We quickly learned that we were in presumption, not
faith. God had a much better plan and we were to learn of
God's timing and purpose. God's plan was for us to move
to Canada two years later! When the time came, the money was there for the tickets and everything fell into place.

To set dates and time lines is not wise. When our hearts
are established in the Word of God, we don't set time lim-
its with God. Our heart is fully assured that what God has

said will come to pass. This gives us such peace and rest.

Learn from disappointments, let the Holy Spirit show you where you missed it. Pick yourself up, dust yourself off, and keep on going and learning this wonderful life of faith and victory. God is never a disappointment, it is impossible for Him to let us down. Trust Him with all your heart!

CLEANSED (CHANGED) BY THE WASHING OF THE WORD
by Michael Nokes

It all began during one of the darkest times of my life, [you know] the kind that makes you just want to curl up and die. The pain in my heart was intense. It felt like my heart was constantly breaking over-and-over and everything I tried, could not stop it.

In my humbled state, I reached out to God and began to read His Word every morning and every night, without fail. It was the first and the last thing I did every single day. I was seeking His face. I am ashamed to say that before this moment, the center of my life was myself and my wife, in that order. One day several months later, I awoke to the revelation that He had changed me from the inside out. I still do not know how he changed my heart. All I can say is: God had been gradually changing me verse by verse and I didn't even notice. He had been cleansing me of all unrighteousness by the washing of the pure water of the Word of God. He changed me into *a new creature* and now I am truly alive!

~

I HEARD IN MY SPIRIT
by Brian Ohse

I was sitting near his desk, as a friend of mine was checking his mail, and as he began to read a postcard advertisement for a upcoming 'Christian Conference'—I heard in my spirit: *"NOT REAL!"* Which my friend confirmed, since he had attended one of this particular organization's conferences in the past.

I haven't had a lot of rest lately, I've had too many things going on. But through it all, I'm being made more sensitive to (hearing and feeling more quickly and clearly) spiritual things. Didn't Paul say, *"In my weakness He is being made strong?"* (cf. 2 Co 12:9) So the weaker I become in the flesh, the stronger I am in spirit.

Even to the point, *words of knowledge* just come to me when I am standing before someone at a store or restaurant. Like the waitress I spoke to by the spirit, that she was an encourager, and that was the reason she was at that job. God was using her, to bring encouragement to others.

I tell you, it's time for The Church to get tuned-up and tuned-in to the Holy Ghost. People need to hear a Word (direction) from the Holy Spirit, like never before. It's time Church.

∾

GUILTY
by Ginny Bridges

"Guilty!" "Guilty!" "Guilty!" they cried.
"Guilty!" "Guilty!" "For this he must die!"
"Crucify!" "Crucify!" "Crucify!" they say.
"Take him to Golgotha!" "Kill him today!"

Politically He was a threat. The priests were so afraid.
And as His popularity grew, an evil plot was laid.

They made one of His own -- poor, short-sighted fool --
Betray Him in Gethsemane. But Judas was just a tool
In the long-before conceived plan of the Most High God
To provide restoration through His Beloved Son's blood.

The governor, the priests—none of them could see
That all of this was necessary. It just had to be.
To satisfy *the penalty* for the sins of all mankind,
This one man must be sacrificed.
But He did not look behind.

For the joy set before Him,

He would endure the shameful death --
Crucifixion on a cross. He could do no less.
His back was torn, the flesh laid bare.
Help for Him? There was none – anywhere.

"Beat Him!" "Kick Him!" "Make Him tote that cross
Up the hill!" What if His blood is spilled!"
"His death will be no loss!"
"Lift Him!" "Hang Him!" "Nail Him to the tree!"
"He's guilty!" ...
Of love ....
In the first degree.

∿

IT'S ALL ABOUT ME!
by Jan Collins

How does one minister to people born as early as the 1980's and especially those born in the Twenty-first Century? There are specific ways in which to approach and speak their language. They may perceive Christians and the Church differently than the way we did at their ages.

Unfortunately, our society has reared a very *narcissistic generation, of which we may or may not have contributed to. If you feel as though you have been or actually are narcissistic in the ways described, repentance is the first step. You may feel called to minister to this group of our society. Because the information in this devotional is a very common way to communicate, it can be effective in witnessing to anyone who needs Jesus.

IT'S ALL ABOUT ME!

Is it really "all about me?" Many people nowadays focus on themselves, no matter what subject it is: physical features, financial, success in business or other subjects. Some get focused on themselves so intently, they become obsessed with their selfishness, often not even realizing it. Recognizing that it is really NOT all about ME, is the first step in turning one's back on narcissism.

One will find there are people who are in worst situations than theirs. For the Christian, turning to meditating, memorizing and focusing on learning scriptures, one can turn "It's all about me" into "It's about HIM." If you as the reader, recognizes this negative attribute in another person- young or old, you may feel called to pray and eventually share scriptures that would be beneficial to them in their walk with God.

When we turn it around and make it "all about God"— Meditate on the One who knows you best! Let your mouth be filled with praises to Him. He is the one who created you and has a plan for your life that ONLY you can fulfill!

When you become a new creation in Christ, He turns your life back into a personal relationship with Jesus

Christ, He can and will make you feel THAT SPECIAL!! It is another step toward wellness of the soul. He fulfills our lives! Show young people how to Trust Him and He will make it about them too!

Meditate on the One who knows you best with these scriptures: *Jeremiah 29:11; Luke 6:45; Psalm 19:14; Psalm 49:3; Psalm 18:28; Ephesians 5:19; James 1: 4; Matthew 7:7; Ephesians 1:18-19; Philippians 3:13.*

*narcissistic – having an excessive or erotic interest in one-self and one's physical appearance. Wrapped in oneself; self-admiring. *Synonyms:* self-absorbed, self-obsessed, conceited, self-centered or egomaniac

GOD STILL HEALS TODAY
by Landon Roy Wright

When Brother Aaron announced that God of the Mountain II was in the works, the Lord was already stirring my spirit about a few topics, but this one wasn't one of them. However, the Lord deserves more glory through this story.

I'm a high school teacher and football coach. On August 31, 2018, we lost a game that I had helped prepare eight weeks for, by one point. After the game, as we were packing up to head back to the school, I noticed a lady sitting down near the stands and another lady panicking, so I walked over to see if I could help.

The panicking lady was asking us to go get the ambulance before they left the stadium, so someone went to try to chase them down. In the meantime, I asked if I could pray with her and she let me. After I prayed for her, she became calm, but moments later she started vomiting. A few moments later, the ambulance showed up and took it from there, so I went about my day.

One week later, during sixth period. I got a knock on my classroom door and it was the lady who was panicking the previous Friday night. She had come to the school to find me and tell me the report.

Her sister (the lady I prayed with) was taken to one of the best hospitals in the area and the doctors ran tests and determined that she had had a brain aneurysm, but the pressure didn't bust the vein and instead went away, which she said is extremely rare. The doctors were in shock because that supposedly almost never happens.

The lady is still walking and talking normally, but was literally moments from possibly dying or her life never being the same again.

God still heals and works miracles! One small act of faith can go a long way!

Two weeks later, I ran into the lady at school again, or so I thought. Turns out, it was her sister, the one I prayed with and she was alive and well and praising God. She looked so much different and healthier from the night I prayed with her, that I didn't realize it was her for a few minutes.

Through talking to her I learned she had been a believer for some time. She said since she was a young girl, she wanted to have a moment with God, where she just knew He was real beyond all doubt. She wanted to have an encounter with Him.

That was her encounter.

Now, she is leading a youth group at her church and continues to testify of God's miracle and His overall goodness!

Not only was that her encounter, the whole thing has been so encouraging to me, because, to my knowledge, that is the most severe thing I've seen the Lord heal through my prayers. I've seen God heal headaches, back aches, acid reflux, dizziness and other things like that, dozens of times with no problem, but this—this is a new level. Now that He's done it, I'm expecting it more and more often.

See when Christ bore our sicknesses *(cf. 1 Peter 2:24)*, it was all of them; they are one in the same, not just the minor ones, but the major ones too. Every single sickness (big or small) has to bow to the Name of Jesus and get out!

∽

MEND AND MAKE GOOD
by Daryl P Holloman

[And we] continue to pray especially and with most intense earnestness night and day that we may see you face to face and mend and make good whatever may be imperfect and lacking in your faith.
— I Thessalonians 3:10 Amplified Bible

Mend – 1: to free from faults or defects: as a: to improve in manners or morals b: to set right c: to put into good shape or working order again d: to restore to health —*Webster's Ninth New Collegiate Dictionary*

Make – 2b: to cause to exist, occur or appear --- Ibid

1 **Good** – 1a: (1) of a favorable character or tendency b: (2) free from injury or disease --- Ibid

2 **Good** – 2: advancement of prosperity or health --- Ibid

Prosperity – the condition of being successful or thriving --- Ibid

We have an assignment as Believers, to help people *grow* and *mature*, both spiritually and naturally, in-line with what is *revealed to us in Scriptures by the Holy Ghost.*

People's lives have been shattered and broken by countless situations and circumstances that invade their lives; both expectedly and [especially] unexpectedly.

Our purpose as Believers is: to learn how to overcome the storms of life with Faith in the Word of God; while learning how to follow the unction and leading of the Holy Spirit. He is the One Who *comforts* and breathes *life* upon the Scriptures we study and meditate upon.

First and foremost, it takes *fervent* and *expectant* prayer that agrees with *the revelation* of the Scriptures to lead Believers to that place in Christ Jesus, where the Anointing and *unction* of the Holy Ghost, makes the Scriptures a *living* and *working reality* in the lives of every Believer.

The combination of our prayers and *the words that we speak,* should *mend and repair* the broken lives that the Holy Spirit brings us in contact with along *the road of life.*

The results of our prayers and *spoken words* should *produce* success and healings in the lives that we pray and *speak Faith-inspired words* into on a daily basis: be it our own lives or the lives of others we meet along the countless paths of life.

Our prayers and spoken words are to *advance* the *success* and *health* of every Believer; as well as the lives of those who do not know Jesus Christ as their personal Lord and Savior.

We must stand in *the gap* for both the Believers [as well as the unbelievers] with our Scripture-based prayers and words of Faith that we speak consistently and without Wavering on a daily basis.

Instead of focusing upon the negative failures and disappointments that invade our lives, the Scriptures and the Holy Ghost will rise up to unction us to attack the negative circumstance with the Faith that has grown in our hearts by studying and meditating upon the Scriptures.

Our assignment from Heaven is to spread encouragement and healing to all broken lives!

~

MYSTERIES OF VICTORY
by Barbara J. White

I heard this phrase recently, "mysteries of victories," as I listened to a podcast and it grabbed my attention. I began to meditate on these words and revelation rose up in my spirit as to their meaning.

God has given His children secret weapons to use in prayer. Besides the use of the Name of Jesus and the Word of God, we have through the power and anointing of the Holy Spirit, the authority to pray in tongues. When we do this, we are releasing divine purposes and plans, God-given answers to our prayers. There are times when *we do not know how to pray as we ought* due to a lack of knowledge *(See: Ro 8:26-27)*. But the Holy Spirit, our Helper, comes to our aid and enables us to pray the mysteries (divine secrets and purposes) of God on behalf of a person or situation.

The mysteries we pray in the Spirit, manifest in glorious answers to prayer. This should rejoice your heart today, knowing you are praying in line with the will of the Father. Results are forthcoming and victories manifesting. Guaranteed!

The enemy may try to convince you that nothing is happening and you are wasting your time praying in tongues. But he is a liar, and his thoughts must be cast down and replaced with God's Word. Your prayer in tongues is very effective, that is why the enemy tries to stop you from praying in this powerful God-given way.

Thank God, He always causes us to triumph in Christ Jesus. Don't stop praying in this manner! The mysteries are turning to victories!

BREAKTHROUGH
by Bruce A. Higgins

As I continued to study and spend time in God's Word, my breakthrough came. It didn't come from what someone said or from what someone else thought; it came from the Word of God and what God said and taught. God's Word actually became *healing* and *medicine* to my flesh.

Proverbs 4:20-22 KJV
20 My son, attend to my words; incline thine ear unto my sayings.
21 Let them not depart from thine eyes; keep them in the midst of thine heart.
22 For they [are] life unto those that find them, and health to all their flesh.

You know, well-meaning people will often tell you things based on past experience, on what they were taught, or on what they think the Word of God says. That's why you have to attend to God's Word. You have to make sure what you're hearing or believing is not based on one isolated Scripture, but is balanced throughout the entire Word of God.

Matthew 18:16 KJV
But if he will not hear [thee, then] take with thee one or two more, that in the mouth of two or three witnesses every word may be established.

No matter who tells you something, whether it's your *Pastor*, Sunday School teacher, television *Evangelist*, or anyone else—don't just blindly accept it as truth, if it doesn't line up with the whole Bible; forget it.

Healing is Already Paid For

My breakthrough came one evening at a Bible study. That night, I received the revelation of a precious verse of Scripture: *"Who [Jesus] his own self bare our sins in his own body on the tree [cross], that we, being dead to sins, should live unto righteousness; by whose stripes [wounds] ye were healed." (1 Peter 2:24)*

Suddenly, it hit me—I didn't have to earn my healing! In fact, my healing [already] *belonged to me,* because of the price Jesus paid on Calvary.

Romans 8:32 RSV
He who did not spare his own Son but gave him up for us all, will he not also give us all things with him?

As I continued to study God's Word, it became even more clear to me, that healing is a gift just like salvation; I couldn't earn it, all I could do was receive it. I didn't need to get healed because healing was mine already. All I had to do was *stand in faith,* and rebuke the devil in Jesus' Name.

James 4:7 KJV
Submit yourselves therefore to God. Resist the devil, and he will flee from you.

CALL THEM BACK
by Kim Wear

Call back the Sinners and Backsliders.

If anyone among you wanders from the truth, and someone turns him back, let him know that he who

*turns a sinner from error of his way will save a soul
from death and cover a multitude of sins.*
– James 5:19-20 NKJV

Many think they are righteous exposing and judging
someone else's sins. But *love,* is the strongest ministry,
and it covers and restores those in sin. That's *the ministry of Christ;* seeking to restore, not expose and condemn.
There are times you must confront, but always in love,
so they feel secure enough in God's love, and yours, to
receive *the ministry of reconciliation.*

When The Church becomes a love ministry, she will
be—A POWERFUL MINISTRY.

∽

ALL
by Adrienne Gottlieb

*"And God is able to make all grace abound to you, that
always having all sufficiency in everything, you may
have an abundance for every good deed"*
– 2 Corinthians 9:8 NASB

First of all, we need to see that the level of God's provision
is abundance. We also need to note that the key to right giving—is grace, which comes only through Jesus, through the
cross; and is received by faith.

There are two key words in the above quoted verse. They are *"all"* and *"abound."* "All" occurs 5 times, "abound" twice. There's no way the language could be more emphatic; to clarify, even though most English translations use the phrase *"every good deed (or work)"* the Greek is *"all"* good deeds.

If you have all that you need in all things at all times to abound to every (all) good work or deed, there is absolutely no room for unsupplied need anywhere in your life!

Now, let's look at the word *"abundance."* In the Latin, it's meaning is, "a wave that overflows." For instance, the Scripture says, *"Out of the abundance of the heart the mouth speaks (or overflows) (See: Mt 12:34)."*

God is not speaking about just enough to get by, He is speaking about providing us with overflowing provisions so that we can overflow in every GOOD deed. If we by faith appropriate His grace, then the level of His provision is abundance. Wow! Does it get any better than that?

Please note: however, that the purpose of His abundance is for us to abound in "every good deed." We are not talking about selfish indulgences. The reason: *"It is more blessed to give than to receive (See: Acts 20:35)."*

Receiving has a blessing, but giving has a greater blessing. God has no favorites among His children. He wants all that are His to enjoy the greater blessing of giving. God makes

His abundance available to us, so that we may not be limited to the blessing of receiving only, but that we may also be in a position to enjoy the greater blessing of giving.

First we give, then we receive. That is faith. Simple? Yes. Then: Why is it so difficult for most of us? Perhaps it's that interval between the sowing and reaping. We in America are so used to wanting and seeing immediate results that we forget what Paul said in *Galatians 6:9: And let us not lose heart in doing good, for in due time we shall reap if we do not grow weary.*

~

ALLOW THE WIND OF THE SPIRIT
TO SET YOUR COURSE
by Pam Tattershall

The Holy Spirit is the *Spirit of God,* the *Wind of God,* and *Breath of God.* In the Hebrew, *ruach* means spirit, wind and breath. The Greek word, *pneuma,* also means spirit, wind and breath. When God formed Adam, it was the breath of God that caused him to live. (*"And the LORD God formed man of the dust of the ground, and breathed into his nostrils the breath of life; and man became a living being" Genesis 2:7).* It is the same Spirit of God that causes us to live this new life when we repent of our sins and accept Jesus, as our Lord and Savior. However, unless we are constantly being replenished with His Life, we soon find that in ourselves our natural reserves are limited. We become exhausted and have nothing more to offer: We are worn out, breathless and winded. Conversely, the opposite effect occurs when the Christian allows the Holy Spirit to direct their life. The Christian's life is lived with purpose, direction and strength because her or his life is yielded to the Spirit of God.

Nearly a half-century ago, a Scottish pastor, James S. Stewart, published a book of sermons that went by the title of the first sermon, "The Wind of the Spirit." His text for that message was something the Lord said to Nicodemus, *"The wind blows where it wishes, and you hear the sound of it, but cannot tell where it comes from and where it goes. So is everyone who is born of the Spirit" (John 3:8).* In my opinion, Stewart's outline on this powerful truth gives us an understanding of the depth of the Lord's teaching about the *Wind of the Spirit.*

"The wind blows"—That bare, simple statement affirms the ceaseless action of the Spirit. Never has there been a time, never a moment, when the Spirit of God has not been actively at work.

"The wind blows where it wishes"—This is the sovereign freedom of the Spirit. Just as it is impossible to control the wind or dictate its direction, so no man, no Church, can domesticate the Spirit of God.

"...and you hear the sound of it"—This is the indisput-

able evidence of the Spirit. He makes Himself evident, His presence felt. You know the living God is at work in this place.

"...but cannot tell where it comes from"—This is the inscrutable origin of the Spirit. We do not know what God has been doing before beginning His work at this point and in this place, only that He has.

"...and where it goes"—This is the incalculable destiny of the Spirit. You cannot tell where He is liable to carry you.

The *Wind of the Spirit* is a resource for believers beyond measure. The Spirit is: God's strength for our weakness, His sight for our blindness, and His supply for our need. He carries us and moves us, even when we do not know that He is at work.

~

THE LIGHT OF THE WORLD
by Jan Collins

A farmer's family had gone to church and left him all alone
Their love for him was very strong,
but his beliefs they could not condone.
He sat in his chair as he watched the flickering fire,
Thinking of his dreams in life,
and wondering what WAS his heart's desire.

The GOD of the MOUNTAIN II

He saw the world as nature, creation all around
But on the ways of God, his mind could not expound.

Mysteriously a sound was made outside in the dark of night
A bird had lost its way, confusion was its plight.
He hurried to the barn and lit a lantern there
He had in mind this little one and its life to spare.

'If I were only a bird myself, I'd guide him down to Earth,
Toward this light, this bird's only hope-
EACH creature has SOME worth',
And just as if a light came on, in his mortal mind
He realized what God had done for all of His mankind.

God came to Earth a man Himself,
as a babe, a beautiful sight,
He came to Earth to show men the way
toward His precious Light!

"I am the Way, the Truth, and the Life. No one comes to the Father except through Me. If you had known Me, you would have known My Father also; and from now on you know Him and have seen Him." – John 14:6 NKJV

"I am the light of the world. Whoever follows me will never walk in darkness, but will have the light of life." – John 8:12 NKJV

~

WORRYING
by Steve Farmer

Sometimes, worrying about "why" something happened, is like being obsessed with "why" your shoes came untied...

"Bend down, retie them, and move on down the road!!!!"

~

OBEDIENCE IS BETTER...
by Brian Ohse
The following exerpt was taken from
"THE KEYS TO UNLOCKING THE DOOR OF VICTORY"
▪ Used by Permission.

Now we'll talk about obedience through serving. Does the Word not say, *"Obedience is better than sacrifice?"* But, what does that mean? Let's find out. Holy Spirit help me to see and receive *revelation* in Jesus' Name; Amen.

When I first began my research, I found out "obey" is really how the Scripture reads. Now listen to what Strong's had to say about *obey*, "hear intelligently, consent, consider, discern, and proclaim." I think of the Scripture, *"They that have an ear to hear, hear what the Spirit has to say."* So you're suppose to hear with your heart and spirit open, then to agree and be of the same mind, then examine for yourself the truth you've heard, and reflect it in your own life. And then, most importantly, you'll be able to discern in your spirit what is man speaking, and what is God. Then after all this, you're to officially proclaim the truth to all God's people. That means both the saved, and unsaved. Now are you beginning to understand His Word more fully? Then hold on, because now we're going to bring this truth home, by looking at the second word *"sacrifice"* in Webster's, that in turn gave me the word *"forfeiture"* which said, *"the act of surrendering something."* Do you get this? You're pretending that you gave something up, but in reality, you gave nothing. Have you ever seen people that go to the altar weeping, yet you still see no change in their life? This is what I'm talking about. I've spoken about this before, but apparently it's supposed to be repeated. *"All we have is a bunch of professional actors in the Body of Christ,"*—no true repenters. So, be one of those that shows what true holiness is all about, hungering for Him and Him alone.

So what's another key? Quick obedience to His Spirit, with a servant's heart. *Deuteronomy chapter 11, verses 13 and 14: "I command you this day to love the Lord your God and to serve Him with all your heart and all your soul."*

Now see the blessing for doing it, in *verse 14, "I will give you the rain of your land in His due season, the first rain and the latter rain, that thou mayest gather in the corn and thy wine and thy oil."* The Holy Spirit impresses me to again *research* the Scripture, so we'll look at, "rain, first, latter,

corn, wine, and oil." But before I get into it, know I'm doing this indepth *study* to learn for myself, what the Spirit
desires to *reveal*. Because there's much truth *hidden* in His
Word. Also, I'm not doing this because of curiousity about
truth, but rather I'm following the prompting of the Holy
Spirit. Now let's get started. As I looked at the word "rain"
in Strong's, I wasn't really surprised to find a different re-
frence number for each one. Which is confirmation there's
something hidden here. Because when we look at the first
part of this Scripture, *"I will give you rain of your land,"*
it's talking about natural rain, the refreshing of the land.
But, when "First rain" is researched, listen to what came
up, *"sprinkling, point out, to teach, inform, and instruct."* So
it's clear here that we're to point people the way, teach them
God's Word, inform them of judgement being put in place
because of wickedness, and then educate, providing them
with knowledge, so they too—can walk in victory.

∾

I SING
by Paul Howard

I sing because I'm happy
I sing because I'm Glad
I know that he is with me
Upheld by his right hand

I think about his goodness
And what He means to me

He's closer that a brother
Even when I'm not in need

I will follow Jesus
The song comes back to me
He is my provider
He supplies my every need

He feeds the crows and birds
I will never hunger be
He's proven that over and over
I will never anxious be

I sing about my Journey
With Him I'm always pleased
He guides my every step
With Him I'll always be

COME INTO THIS PLACE
by Rachel V. Jeffries

There is a place in God, where we can come and be sheltered. So many Scriptures talk about us coming into that place. Old hymns were written about *"He Hideth My Soul in the Cleft of the Rock. He shadows the dry thirsty land. He covers my life with the depths of His Love and covers me there with His hand."* These are all words written a long time ago. God knows just exactly what is being done today in our governments, our banking system, and in our families. We are dealing with issues today, we would have never dreamed of in years past.

LOVE OF GOD OVERWHELMING YOU

I found a note this morning which I had written April 11, 2013, while recording the song on the CD, "*Come Into This Place.*" I felt like weeping because of the presence of God. Some words in the song say, "*Jesus, You I Adore.*" When I sang that, I could not hold back the tears. God's love for the listeners overwhelmed me and everyone in the studio. He spoke to me about my desire for the AMAZING LOVE CD, *[See ad on page 216]* that people would be rising above what is wrong in the world, and in their lives. I had asked that those who had not experienced Jesus would be drawn to Him. At that point, I spoke in tongues and the interpretation was, "*What is in your heart for this CD shall come to pass.*"

FULFILLMENT OF VISION

When I mention this CD, it is a fulfillment of what I have in my heart for God's people. You may have asked Jesus into your life, but your fellowship with Him may be shallow. When you get into His presence, it is so different. This song invites you in, it was written by *inspiration* of the Holy Spirit. *Come Into This Place.* There is a *place* where we can hide in Him. WORSHIP HIM IN THAT PLACE.

PRAYER: Lord, I need your presence in my life. Help me to come into that place, where the world cannot contest what You have done in me. I come behind that inner veil that You have rent in two. Jesus, You I adore. I tell You today, I truly love You. Saturate me with Your presence, where there is fullness of joy. AMEN!

CONFESSION: I am not afraid to allow the presence of God to touch my life in every area. I trust in Him. I receive His love without hesitation. I am not a beggar always trying to manipulate God to get something. I truly love Him and He produces in my life. He brings substance. I serve God, because I truly love fellowshiping with the Father, Son and the Holy Spirit. HALLELUJAH!

BOOK OF HEZEKIAH
by Marcella O'Banion Burnes

*Book of Hezekiah
Prophet Jeremiah

Read on the pages
Story of the Ages

You doubt? You shout.
Be Warned
Faith was born.

Nehemiah on the wall
Jonah did fall

The GOD of the MOUNTAIN II

Goliath turned to Rattle
David Didn't Get Addled

Ruth was no Kin
But with Boaz she did win

There lepers at the gate
For great rewards they weren't late

Achin Hid his sin
Judgement came for him

Samson in his final hour
God granted tremendous power

Trapped with some lions
Daniel wasn't crying

Meshack, Shadrack, Abednego
In the fire they did go

Elijah sitting on a funeral pyre
Demanded they soak the wood with water for fire

James, Peter, and John
Watched the Master walk the water on

Apostles casting nets from their boats
Gigantic loads of fish did float

The Master of the sea
Bid Peter come on the water to He

Noah Built a Giant Boat
Not knowing it would float

Gideon broke the pitcher and bowl
Blowing the horn for the battle to go

In each and every story
Faith waked for God's Glory

Time and time again
In faithfulness God gave the win

Each and every time
God's Glory did shine

No matter what the occasion
God showed out for his ovation

Master of it all
He know everyone and everyone he calls

Run to HIM every time
trust in Him and HIS GLORY WILL SHINE

Book of Proverbs from Solomon was published under King Hezekiah's reign thus known as Book of Hezekiah.

PROTECT THE ANOINTING ON YOUR LIFE
by Barbara J. White

The attacks on our *spirit, soul,* and *body* will come, so don't be surprised when they appear. I want to specifically address the attacks by the enemy concerning the anointing of the Holy Spirit on our lives, homes, families, businesses and ministries.

Peter says to *"think it not strange – amazed and bewildered – when the fiery trails come." (See: 2 Pe 4:12)* And we know God does not send them. *(cf. Ja 1:13)* Every believer has received an anointing on their lives, *(cf. 1 Jo 2:20)* so don't be disturbed when the anointing is attacked. *The plan* of the enemy is to diminish the anointing given to us by the Holy Spirit. His strategy is to keep us ineffective through various means. The Holy Spirit has empowered us to be witnesses here on the earth, with access to His teaching ministry. He brings revelation, knowledge, and understanding to our heart and mind.

The first sign that the anointing is under attack is: our vision becomes blurry and less real. God's will is that the eyes of our understanding are enlightened and that we know the hope of our calling *(See: Eph 1:18)*. Keeping God's plan and purpose before our eyes and in our heart will preserve our godly vision for our life.

One *strategy* of the enemy is to minimize our real value in God. Words received from others, and Satan himself, will cause us to lose our identity in Jesus. Circumstances, can shout *negative words* and create foreboding thoughts, that will tempt us to agree with what has been said. He will tempt us to look at our circumstances, instead of the Truth; God's Word. We must stop the enemy in his tracks, get right back on the Word of God, boldly declaring who we are in Christ, and what—we can do in HIM!

If we follow God's plan with limited vision and receive

words contrary to the will of God, we will lose our Holy Spirit *momentum*. We will find ourselves bound in *fear,* and any movement forward in faith will be difficult.

Lastly, we will find our work, ministry, and everything we attempt, will become nothing but a monotonous grind! The joy that resides in our spirit will be suppressed. This is not the will of God.

Believers, rise up and shake off the lies of the adversary with *boldness* and *confidence* in your position in Jesus. You have been raised up to sit together with Him in the heavenly realm, and how dare the enemy attack you! Rise up, and shake off every encumbrance—boldly move forward. The *joy* will rise within your spirit and you will be strengthened to move forward in *faith* and *victory.*

~

FAITHFUL IN A VERY LITTLE
by Mike Harris

According to *Luke 2, verse 8* there were some faithful shepherds just doing their job. *"And there were in the same country shepherds abiding in the field, keeping watch over their flocks by night."* These shepherds had the night shift, and could not have known they would divinely be included as witnesses to the most awesome world changing event in history; after all, they were just being faithful, abiding in the field on yet another starry night. It all started the same as the night before or any other night. There was no special invitation extended, nothing that would entice them to show up that night for their normal duties of tending sheep; but then, according to *verse 9*, *"... the angel of the Lord came upon them, and the glory of the Lord shone round about them..."* and everything changed.

Faithfulness in the least, puts us in a position of promotion. It was Jesus Who said, *"He that is faithful in that which is least is faithful also in much..."* And the shepherds on that special night were proof that the little things really do matter. Little things like being on time. ...What if everyone gave attention to such small matters?

Later in *chapter 19* we find Christ teaching, where we read about a good servant. Jesus calls this servant *"good"* because he has been faithful in a very little *(v 17)*. Notice that Jesus went on to promote the "good" servant, by making him ruler over ten cities. Now that is no small promotion. It also seems, that advancement comes when we least expect it. The promotion comes when we have been faithful in the very little, the things that we think are not even noticed.

The Prophet Zechariah said in *chapter 4, verse 10*, *"For who hath despised the day of small things."* And Solomon exhorted us, to take care of the little things—for they are what spoil the vines.

I pray for you to be encouraged today and remain faithful in all that you have been given. May His strength rise up within you, that hope will abound, and everything you find to do will be done with all your heart and soul; not as pleasing unto men, but pleasing to God.

So, don't grow weary, the harvest will come.

PLANTED TO PRODUCE
by Aaron Jones

Luke 13:6-9 (Plain English Bible)
6 And he told this *parable: "A man had a fig tree that was planted in his vineyard and he came seeking fruit on it and he found none.
7 And he said to the cultivator, 'Behold, three years I have come seeking fruit in this fig tree, and I find none; cut it down; why is it taking up space?'
8 The cultivator said to him, 'My Lord, leave it also this year, while I shall cultivate it and I shall manure it',
9 And perhaps it will have borne fruit, otherwise next year you should cut it down."

*parable - a simple story illustrating a moral or spiritual truth.

Let's bring this a little [okay a lot] closer.

Luke 13:6-9 (pp)
6 And Jesus revealed this spiritual truth in the form

of a story: "God had a Christian planted on His prop-
erty and He came expecting him to have done some-
thing for The Kingdom, but he hadn't yet.
7 And God said to the Holy Ghost, "Look, I've watched
this one for some time expecting him to produce fruit
for My Kingdom, but still nothing; remove him, why
is he wasting this life?"
8 The Holy Ghost made intercession for him to God,
"My Lord, don't bring judgement yet, but be patient
another year, and I will shake up and turn over every-
thing around him and I will put more crap on him."
9 Then maybe he will produce something for Heaven,
if after I have dealt with him he still doesn't produce
then send judgement.

As a Christian, I know I have believed God, named it and
claimed it, blabbed it and grabbed it, confessed and believed, etc... and still, it just seemed like more 'manure'
kept happening to me. Have you been there? Look around
you: Is the everything being tore up, are you in deep stuff
right now?

Often, (Christians) need to be reminded this walk is
about His Kingdom—not ours! In this life, we get way
too busy taking care of every day tasks, working to make
ends meet, instead of working as if there is an eternal destiny we all will meet. There is a real danger, that many
may be caught doing 'good things' and not 'God things,'
when He comes!

Natural trees don't produce *eternal fruits*. Only *trees planted of the Lord* are capable of producing this precious fruit—and God does expect it! We cannot be planted in The Kingdom, and stand around non-productive (looking like worldly trees.)

John 15:1-5 KJV
1 I am the true vine, and my Father is the husbandman.
2 Every branch in me that beareth not fruit he taketh away: and every branch that beareth fruit, he purgeth it, that it may bring forth more fruit.
3 Now ye are clean through the word which I have spoken unto you.
4 Abide in me, and I in you. As the branch cannot bear fruit of itself, except it abide in the vine; no more can ye, except ye abide in me.
5 I am the vine, ye are the branches: He that abideth in me, and I in him, the same bringeth forth much fruit: for without me ye can do nothing.

~

I GAVE UP
by Shawn Scheffler

"I gave up!" After months of trying I just couldn't take it anymore. Sound familiar? I tried, really, I did try. No one noticed. I am not even sure that anyone cared. Then it resounded within me that something had to be done. What

should I do with all this information I had obtained? I was on overload and my mind felt like mush.

Today, in just one of my email accounts I searched one person's name and had over 5557 emails since July of 2014. This didn't count all the replies. Each email contained ideas on how to make more money by doing this or that. Each email had a link, a success story, and yet another method. I finished spending a few hours online trying to see how I could do it again.

Two stories come to mind in regard to this point. Several years ago, I had a co-worker and great friend who froze right in the middle of trying to pursue their dream career. Thousands of hours and money of course and they froze. The pressure became so great, that the thought of another semester of college made this person sick. Information overload caused them to tilt.

The second story is very personal. At the age of 9, I knew I wanted to write books. When I was in Bible College the idea came to me for my very first book. I had the outline and could even see myself helping train others with it. The only problem I had was, *"I gave up."* I kept those thoughts and ideas to myself and the outline stayed in the folder I tucked it into.

Life happened and before I knew it, the desire to write had faded away, or so I thought. In a short period of time, my entire life turned upside down. My family was no longer a family and 1 of our 5 was gone to another place. I had written the rough draft of my book right before this happened. After completing it, life happened again, but this time it was my wife who had gone to another place. When that happened, no book seemed valuable. I set it aside and gave up.

True to my own word: *Learning is valuable.* However, there comes a point in which you must start applying all that knowledge and do something about it.

I found that I had come to the point, where I had to apply what I knew and do something with it.

I challenge you today, to start doing what you already know to do and watch it make things change.

THE REVOLT
by Daryl P Holloman

No one noticed the blip on the radar as a foreign object passed through the slight tear in the fabric of time and space.

No one noticed how the remote mountains swallowed up any trace of the aforementioned foreign object as it crash-landed in a sparsely populated territory, where some people had migrated over the centuries to disappear from the prying eyes of civilization.

No human bore witness to the crash-landing of the alien spacecraft and no animal was sent to spread the alarm of an alien invader in their habitat.

Fortunately, for the alien humanoid, whether by divine intervention or freak happenstance, there was an abandoned cabin in this remote wilderness, where he could tend to his wounds, once he had extricated himself from the twisted wreckage of his royal fighter-pod.

Rann Garr had managed to survive the sneak attack of the rebel minions of his ruthless brother Sinn Garr by teleporting his fighter-pod through the very fabric of space and time via his dimensional teleporter.

Said teleporter had sent a secret signal to his royal garrison, so it would only be a matter of time before Rann Garr would be rescued from this back-water planet upon which the royal ruler was now seemingly stranded.

He had enough technology and weaponry to heal his wounds and secure plenty of nourishing meat from the surrounding wildlife to sustain him until he was rescued by one or more of his loyal royal troopers.

Inside the cabin, Rann Garr was able to find a bit of suitable comfort and shelter in the primitive abode, along with a curious leather-worn book, that served to pass the time of his forced exile over the next several weeks.

The advanced technology from his native planet allowed the alien ruler to decipher and come to an understanding of the written words on the well-worn pages of the book that was recorded in a foreign tongue.

The weeks passed quickly and Rann Garr was rescued by his loyal royal troopers without any evidence to the inhabitants of this backwater planet that he or his damaged vessel had ever been present in this remote territory.

In his absence, Sinn Garr had been apprehended and all of his followers were in custody, awaiting the order of execution from his royal sibling.

Rann Garr passed judgement that his rebellious brother would be sentenced to learn what he had learned from that old well-worn book and that his life would be spared and his treason forgiven.

He had shown mercy, by doing the Words revealed to him in the pages of that leather-worn Book.

> *25 And whenever you stand praying, if you have anything against anyone, forgive him and let it drop (leave it, let it go), in order that your Father Who is in Heaven, may also forgive you your [own] failings and shortcomings, and let them drop.*
> *26 But if you do not forgive, neither will your Father in heaven forgive your failings and shortcomings.*
> *– Mark 11:25-26 AMP*

∼

PSALM 116:15
by Len Blanchard

I was sitting on the counter in the Fellowship Hall of the Church I was pastoring. I was told that we had a young man that wanted to play on our ball team. He was going to come to our meeting that evening and that if we let him play, he would be the fastest guy on our team. We already had two of the fastest guys I had ever played with so I was just a little skeptical. Then, he walked in and I almost fell off the counter laughing, but I kept silent as to why I was laughing so hard. He was 5' 9" tall and weighed 265 pounds: You tell me what you would have thought? His name was Donnie Smith and, [you guessed it] he was indeed the fastest man on the team; incredible! God had gifted this young man as a great football player and was an all-around good guy, but... with some issues.

Donnie was saved and when I say he was saved, I mean he got ALL OF JESUS. So radically transformed, that his friends were stunned. He was indeed peculiar. He wanted to win people to this Jesus he had found, and indeed he did win some. What happened a few months later could only be described as a "Jesus work."

In a few short months I received a horrible call. Donnie was an iron worker and had fallen on his job from, [I believe] 28 feet to his death. I sped the two hours to the hospital where he was. As I got there, I was reminded of something I had read as I saw a large crowd standing around the ER door. "NEEDED! Men! Real Men! None else need apply!" There were these tough looking iron workers standing all around. I saw all their eyes turn to me as I entered. I was the "Preacher" where this guy had gone to church and had so much of a life change. One would later tell me they wondered what I would say and how I would handle this.

His desire to "win people to Jesus" was so short-lived, or so we thought. How would you measure such a short-lived time to one so gloriously saved? The week after the funeral there were two new families at the church. The next week, three more families. All of them were saved. On and on it went for nearly a year, each of them testifying to the wonderful life of Donnie Smith.

Oh, in this "Jesus work" Heaven is much brighter and will be filled with families that Donnie touched for the Glory of God.

Psalm 116:15 KJV
Precious in the sight of the Lord is the death of his saints.

~

THE SPIRIT OF PROPHECY
by Barbara J. White

Prophecy, is one of the nine gifts of the Holy Spirit as listed in *1 Corinthians 12:7-10.* Every manifestation of the Spirit is for the profit of The Church, bringing great comfort, edification and exhortation. *(See: 1 Co 14:3)* The ministry of the Spirit is always to bring blessing and edification to God's people. It is never to tear down, criticize or condemn. True prophetic utterance lifts the believer up and sets his heart aglow with hope and a refreshing.

I was again reminded of the tremendous power and anointing released through *the gift of prophecy.* When I minister in the prophetic each person who receives the "word of the Lord" is quickened, encouraged and equipped to fight the good fight of faith. *(e.g. 1 Ti 1:18)*

Revelation 19:10 gives us further insight into this wonderful, supernatural gift. The spirit of prophecy is the testimony of Jesus. It will always bring glory to Jesus, and speak of His wonderful works and plans for His children.

There is a warning in *1 Thessalonians 5:19 and 20* to not suppress the Holy Spirit, especially the gifts and *utterances* of the prophets; to put it differently, do not depreciate prophetic revelations, nor despise inspired instruction or exhortation.

This is again emphasized in *Psalm 19:10 AMP*, where David wrote: *"The law of the Lord is perfect, restoring the [whole] person; the testimony of the Lord is sure, making wise the simple."* The testimony of the Lord is "the spirit of prophecy" as confirmed in *Revelation 19:10*.

The *"word of the Lord,"* given in a prophetic word under the anointing of the Holy Spirit, is precious and valuable to the believer. Often the gifts of *the word of wisdom* and *the word of knowledge* flow within the prophetic utterance. A prophetic word can supernaturally lift the spirit of a believer. The manifested awareness of God's presence, is like a surge of God's power, enlightening the eyes of our understanding.

The church was birthed in the power of the Holy Spirit on the day of Pentecost, and it is God's will for us to flow in His mighty anointing through the gifts of the Holy Spirit.

We are instructed in *1 Corinthians 14:39 AMP* to *"earnestly desire and set our hearts on prophesying."* Thank God for this wonderful gift that glorifies Jesus!

FAITH—THE GREATEST GIFT OF ALL
by Michael Nokes
"Dedicated to Sunshine Leigh"

When faith was lacking, perhaps missing completely, I didn't even understand what it was. I understood in part.

In fact, I wouldn't have been able to describe it back then, at least not the way God knows it. There is no earthly way! It would have been impossible. Because it was Heavenly! After it was bestowed upon me, the scriptural truth was in-my-face apparent. It became so simple and so plain, whereas before it was hidden. As a boy, I had been taught that the more times I heard the word, the stronger my faith would be. When He gave it to me, it was absolutely *a gift*, all of a sudden the scriptural truth was revealed. The truth was in-the-pages the entire time, but only with God's help was I gifted to understand.

This is what was revealed: *faith* is a gift, lest any of mankind should boast. *He is our source of all.* All glory is His. Faith is the *"substance"* of things hoped for, the *evidence* or *proof* of things unseen. Faith is more than fleshly confidence; it is confidence of the God-kind. That means when faith is truly present the supernatural is *"manifested"* into the world of the flesh. *Hebrews 11:1-3* is clear in the King James Version. Where faith is, you will see miracles.

But, until then God is the Judge of the thoughts and intents of the heart. It is a matter of purity, a matter of the heart, and a matter of your diligence!

Personally, I prefer the KJV Bible. Other versions attempt to clarify the meaning of the Scriptures, but only seem to water them down by trying to define heavenly things by earthly standards. Their own understanding gets in the way. One version does not state that when faith is present the "supernatural happens," instead, it puts it in terms of theory or feelings. When faith is present, you don't have to will yourself into believing. When you describe faith in terms of "substance" and "evidence" as the King James does, there is now no mistaking the meaning. The KJV emphatically says that when faith is present supernatural things prove of God's existence.

Let's look at *Romans 10:17*.

> *So then faith [cometh] by hearing, and hearing by the word of God.*

The important part is not before the comma, but after. Faith does come by hearing: But, what is hearing? It's more than repetition; in fact, I do not believe it is repetition at all. Not that hearing the Word repetitively is a bad thing, how else do we study the Word (to rightly divide it)? *Hearing,* is referring to understanding or receiving! So, faith comes by hearing, understanding or our ability to receive. Who can receive something they do not understand? And it is impossible for us to understand the things of God on our own. His ways are so much higher than ours. So we do not lean on our own understanding, we learn to lean on His, revealed by the Spirit. We learn to distrust our flesh and trust Him instead. This is why our very ability to understand is unlocked when spiritual blindness falls from our eyes. He is the life-giver! He is the One Who causes the blind to see!

Now let's look at the last half of *Romans 10:17, "..., and hearing by the word of God."* I think its plain enough to determine if the word "cometh" is before the comma, it can be put after the comma as well. So, ...hearing comes by the Word of God and understanding comes by the Word also. So, the Author and Finisher of our faith gives us understanding. He is the Word of God made flesh! Wow, He is still teaching us through the Holy Spirit, Who was sent in His Name.

The scales falling from Saul's eyes and the deaf ears being opened in *Psalm 40:6* are examples of this gift being bestowed. So you can see that since God opens eyes and ears, then faith is a gift, unless a person would have pride to boast of themselves. God embraces the humble, but resists the proud. And all glory belongs to the Father of glory!

WHO CAN BE AGAINST US?
by Wayne Sanders

Romans 8:31 NIV
"What, then, shall we say in response to this? If God is for us, who can be against us?"

I am one of those who is always looking forward with great anticipation to what lies ahead of us as people of God.

We are told to be encouraged for the presence of God is with us, and in us, as we go through our daily affairs in this life.

So, if God be for us, who and what could be against us? Check this out, with God on your side, who in the world can come and defeat you? No one and nothing!

One day I was feeling very depressed and the Lord begin to deal with me. I began to see that if the devil is here, attempting to attack me in my weakest moments and God is with me at that same moment, then why should I be afraid?

The devil has already been defeated! (I thought that I would bring this up to you just in case you didn't already know this.) Why should I fear a defeated foe?

> *Psalm 61:1-2 KJV*
> *1 "Hear my cry, O God; attend to my prayer.*
> *2 From the end of the earth I will cry to You, When my heart is overwhelmed; Lead me to the rock that is higher than I. For You have been a shelter for me, A strong tower from the enemy.... I will trust in the shelter of Your wings."*

I would like to take time to quote a pastor here that sums it up for me very well:

"Christians, it's time for us to move out from this life of fear, this life of being intimidated by this world, it's time for us to move out from a life of worry about tomorrow... it's time for us to move out from this life of not trusting God who has all power and authority in this world... It's time that we start believing what God has told us in His

Word…. He is the King, He is on our side, *"He who did not spare His own Son, but gave him up for us all… how will he not also graciously give us all things?*

"How will we become The Church and the people that God has called us to become? By this, we will believe what He says, and we will live our lives with a confidence of who we are and what we are with Christ living through us with His Resurrection power."

Well put pastor!

I thank you Father for giving me the power to push through to the victory, that is waiting for me on the other side of this battle. You are my strong tower, my present help in times of trouble. My soul rest in you and in the power of your word over my life, Amen.

HEAR AND OBEY
by Sharon Andrews

Acts 19:11-12 KJV
11 And God wrought special miracles by the hands of Paul:
12 So that from his body were brought unto the sick handkerchiefs or aprons, and the diseases departed from them, and the evil spirits went out of them.

I had been to the beauty shop, and was not satisfied how

my hair looked when I got home. I was preparing for a meeting in a couple of days, and needed my hair redone. I prayed and asked the Lord where to go since I wasn't satisfied. The Holy Spirit directed me to go back to my beautician and take a prayer cloth. I thought to myself, *"How can I go back?"* But, I obeyed and set the appointment. I was on my way out the door and my husband said, *"Take a prayer cloth with you, and give it to the beautician."* I said I was—confirmation was given to take her a prayer cloth.

My beautician was gracious and knew what to do to correct my hair.

I waited for the right moment to give her the prayer cloth, I didn't even know if she knew what it was or how she believed.

I handed her the prayer cloth, along with Scriptures on what it was, and some healing Scriptures. I was not aware of any of her health issues at the time.

She grabbed the prayer cloth, and said, she knew what it was for.

I found out that she had a tumor in her ears and nasal cavity, that was only visible when the doctors looked in her ears and nose. She was pregnant at the time, and they wanted her to abort the baby, so she could have the surgery.

She told them she would not have the surgery until after she delivered. The tumor kept growing, and it was now life-threatening; in addition, there were complications during the pregnancy. But each time the prayer cloth was near her body—the complications left.

She delivered her baby against all odds. Then she was scheduled for surgery, and the doctors prepared her for the worst. She said she wanted her prayer cloth left on her when she went into surgery. After she had the surgery, the doctors came out and said the tumors were gone when they went to remove them. All that was left were the empty areas where the tumors had been. Much to the doctors' amazement, she went home that day; God had intervened and healed her through an anointed prayer cloth.

I had given her a small piece of a handkerchief (prayer cloth), which she held onto it. God miraculously delivered her, and she began to tell those with sickness and disease, how she was healed from tumors, and about God working through the prayer cloth. She told us there were 21 people healed of cancer when she gave them a small piece of the prayer cloth and the healing Scriptures.

She said the prayer cloth seemed to multiply like the loaves and fishes, because the cloth really was not that big.

I'm grateful for the leadings of the Holy Spirit. To God be all the glory for His mercy to touch and heal lives.

THE QUIET MAN
by Paul Howard

He was a quiet man,
Never spoke much in a crowd;
When he began to speak
they all gathered round.

Wisdom from this man
Eloquently flowed.
He always pointed to Jesus
—His life he owed.

He was always trusted
To steer you the right way,
He lived for Jesus;
Until his last day.

When he left this world,
People came from far and wide
To celebrate his leaving.
He now lives on the other side.

Most were not worried,
They knew they would see him again.
They too live for Jesus
(The Man Who knew no sin).

I long to see his face,
Hear him say hello;
I will live for Jesus
While I'm here below.

I know I'll see the quiet man
When to Heaven I go!

~

THE SHAMUS
by Daryl P Holloman

The old janitor methodically swept the floor of the old church sanctuary, as he quietly prayed and listened for the familiar voice to speak and give instructions to his inner man.

His Bible lay open on the altar and every few minutes he would read Scriptures and pray to his Heavenly Father in line with the very Scriptures he was reading and meditating upon in his heart.

The still small Voice of the Holy Spirit bearing witness with his spirit, brought the illumination of the Word of God working in harmony and unison with the Spirit of God into the hidden man of his heart.

He reflected upon recent events and things that had happened over the years, where the Holy Ghost had revealed by a Word of Knowledge, the whereabouts of a lost kitten.

The delight of the joy that sprang forth from the face of the little girl, when he had rescued said kitten and brought it safely back to her home unharmed.

That simple act of obedience, had led to another victory of locating a lost little boy in the nearby woods, when others had failed to find any trace of the lost boy.

It was reward enough to see the joy restored to a grieving mother, but he humbly accepted an invitation to a dinner celebration, and a subsequent invitation each year thereafter, to attend a birthday dinner as the boy grew older. Then finally, after graduating high school, another before answering the call to serve his country in the armed forces in a rescue unit.

Not to mention, after a time of prayer, how he saw in a vision the location of a missing diamond ring and politely suggested to the distraught parishioner to check behind a certain drawer, where the missing ring may have fallen.

When the parishioner looked behind the drawer, the missing diamond ring was there.

This is how the old janitor developed the reputation of being a spiritual shamus, or private detective, by the revelations of *the Word of Knowledge* given to him by inspiration of the Spirit of God.

Especially, when a missing set of keys was revealed to be

in a certain businessman's rarely used suit, in a closet full of suits. The janitor commanded his angels to restore the keys and put them in a place where the businessman would realize that only an angel of the Lord could have placed them there. Thus the businessman would know that God had sent an angel to return the lost keys.

The old janitor always made sure that he gave thanks to the Lord and glory to God for these remarkable events, instead of taking all the credit for himself.

So it is with yourselves; since you are so eager and ambitious to possess spiritual endowments and manifestations of the [Holy] Spirit, [concentrate on] striving to excel and to abound [in them] in ways that will build up the church. – I Corinthians 14:12 AMP

THE LIGHT
by Jan Collins

The farmer held the horses' reins
while his wife set her pies and cakes in the wagon;
The rest of his family was getting ready
for the Christmas eve services at church.
Their marriage of several years
yielded a nonverbal communication.
He wanted to deny the truth,
but knowing that he would not be attending…. again.

He facial features bore his independent, stubborn will;
Having a logical mind, that demanded practical answers;
He wouldn't believe 'just any ol' thing',
He helped his wife into the wagon,
as the kids all climbed aboard

She wanted him to go, he knew that well;
He knew her emotions were mixed with sadness,
yet strong faith.
A patient woman, she never pushed, pleaded or preached.
As the others left, he turned back toward the house,
reflecting on the love in her eyes-
his thoughts carefully weighed.

As he watched the flickering fire make colorful flames,
a noise was heard at the window.
A bird had lost its way in the night, but the brightness
inside caused him to flutter against the glass.
He hurried out to the barn, and lit a lantern inside.
Opening the barn doors wide, he hoped to save this little
one from the darkness and cold.

When the bird would not fly toward the barn,
he tried in vain to think of another way.
"If only I were a bird myself. I could fly up and guide him
toward his only hope. Now he is too far away,
to ever see the light again."
And just as if a light came on in his mind,
and sunk deep into his heart, he knew
That's what God did for mankind. He became a man him-

self to show all mankind the way toward His Light.

"I am the Way, the Truth, and the Life... " John 14:6
"I am the light of the world..." John 8:12

~

NOT JUST ANOTHER BOOK
by Aaron Jones

Too many people, treat the Bible as if it's just another book. Like it is some story book that tells the history of a land far, far away, of a culture and people somewhere in our distant past. Sadly, this creates a belief pattern in which God (if there really is one), is also seen as far, far away, out in the cosmos and has little to do with us human beings.

Some consider it a book of religious theology or moral and social philosophy, still others, see it as a literary masterpiece to be preserved, collected, and shelved along with other books, like: 'War and Peace'; 'Shakespeare'; 'Don Quixote'; 'The Qur'an'; and 'The Works of Confucius.'

But nothing could be further from the truth.

The great Dwight L. Moody said, *"The Scriptures are given not to increase our knowledge, but to change our lives."*

Speaking of people in the last days [this time], the Apostle Paul told Timothy, there would be people: *"Having a form of godliness, but denying the power thereof: from such turn away." (2 Timothy 3:5 KJV)*

In other words, these people Paul is referring to, dress like they are godly, they talk and act like they are godly, they do 'some' acts of benevolence in the community or make charitable contributions like [they think] God would do. But in reality, they do not believe The Bible (God's Word) has the power to change or impact their lives on a daily basis. Even though The Bible is God's written will, and was created to be the final authority in every area of life. When faced with situations and pressure, most people believe their senses, they look at the natural, and choose logic and human reasoning over The Scriptures. Or even worse, they choose to listen to the 'experts', i.e., doctors, lawyers, the News, their banker, etc. over what the Word of God tells them.

Understand, we thank God for these professionals and all of their expertise and training; but, we never as believers allow their report to trump *the report of the Lord* (the Word of God). *(cf. Is 53:1)*

Brother Kenneth E Hagin would always say, *"Just read the Bible and act like it is so."*

In the face of symptoms of sickness and disease believe The Bible. If there is a shortage or lack in your finances, believe The Bible, when storms come believe The Bible. God's Word, promises healing and provision if you will only believe it. The power to bring it to pass in your daily life, is already built into The Word—every verse is God-breathed and loaded with life-changing power, if you will only believe.

It is not just another book, it is—The Word of God sent to mankind for our good. It is full of life, full of promises, and full of power. Yes, there are some very serious DON'TS in there, but then, there are just as many, and more wonderful DO'S to be followed and enjoyed.

In the Book of Joshua, God makes this incredible statement of promise.

Joshua 1:8 KJV
This book of the law shall not depart out of thy mouth; but thou shalt meditate therein day and night, that thou mayest observe to do according to all that is written therein: <u>for then thou shalt make thy way prosperous, and then thou shalt have good success.</u>

READ YOUR BIBLE!

TIME
by Marcella O'Banion Burnes

Time
For us to awake, oh church!
For the hour is late
Time

For us to cast off our restraint
Loose the bands from around thy neck
Arise oh sleeper and give no rest.
No more emptiness and vain replies
To souls waiting for the harrow of the skies.
Reaping where thou has not sown
Gathering all who are JESUS' own.
A great end reaping has begun
Will you
Be one of the ones,
Who fills the empty seats
Gives bread to the weak?
Hungry souls our hands await
A feeding from the Master's plate.
Will you
Be one who seals their fate?
Forging bridges across and above
Will you
Be one who shows HIS love?
Time is
Ticking …………
Ticking………..
Fields are white as snow
Harvest is heavy and ready to go.
Reapers needed sure and steady
The wages for all are the same
For the sinner there will be great gain!!!

Lift up your eyes and look on the fields for they are white already to harvest. – John 4:35b KJV

~

NOT LOOKING BACK
by Brian Ohse

This area has to do with staying on the straight and narrow path. In other words, not looking back to the old lifestyle. Because there's nothing to return to; the old you died. So burn bridges, so you can't return. What do I mean? Let the people know that was from your past, you're a Christian now, and you no longer desire the darkness. That is: the getting high, the wild beer bashes where you can't remember who you were with, even that girl that loved to get high and then have sex. Those were the crazy dumb days before you got your heart set right. Now, let's look at the Scripture in *1st Kings chapter 22, verse 43, "The high places were not taken away, for the people offered and burnt incense yet in the high places."* Do you see here, that a place was left for them to return to their old ways? And it was the leaders' responsibility to remove it, but they failed. People, we can do nothing but move forward in Him. There's nothing in the world for us; so, why look to it? Even now His Spirit sits so heavy on me, I want to cry, not because of sadness though, but because of hunger for more of Him.

I tell you, He's given me such revelation about His Word, it overwhelms.

~

FIGHT THE GOOD FIGHT
by Collene Martin

The following exerpt was taken from
"POKING HOLES IN THE DARKNESS"

▪ Used by Permission.

While we were gone to see family, I received a call on my cell phone from a young man I met at Walmart. He would come through my line every now and then and had quite a struggle there for a while. He had walked close with the Lord and he began to get sick and attack after attack dragged him down.

The caller had been warring for someone he didn't even know. A young woman had been shot with a shotgun and the Lord put such a burden on him that he could not even leave his house until he was released by the Lord. When he called me, I was sitting in the living room of my niece, who was preparing supper for us in Lake Charles, Louisiana. He was so excited. He had been praying for two days and calling in troops to be in corporate agreement with him.

This is a man who had been tossed to and fro by sickness, divorce and had been veritably isolated from people. He could not work because he was attacked by illness when he least expected it. He finally got disability and was able to get his groceries, but to others all this would seem as if he wasn't doing what the Lord wanted and he was being punished. I would compare this to a molding and making, a trying of his faith, if you will. He sounded as if he were going through the Job syndrome.

Now I know people don't always look at things like I do, but there have been times when I have been there and the weight of my situations lay heavily on me, to a disastrous degree of pain. I never lost my smile, because—I know Who my Redeemer is. He has always been in the business of rescuing me, just as he did this young man.

My friend told me he had really needed to go to town, but when he heard about this young mother, in serious condition, with two or three children, God put her on his heart as a prayer warrior. Once he began, he could not stop. When he heard that she was out of danger, the Lord released him from his vigil.

How awesome to have God assign someone to you when you don't even know them. I have even heard of God sending someone to tell a saint the answer to a prayer from a dream in the last year. The woman had been praying for her grandson who was having seizures and she was travailing, weeping intensely to the point of pain in her own body, so severely over the young child. The Lord sent a man in her dreams to tell her that it was the paint glue the child was working with to build his models. With that assurance, she called her son and asked him if her grandson was building models and to ask the doctors to check for allergies to the glue; and they were able to bring the seizures under control.

If you have a battle going on in your life, God has the answer. All those years of mom and dad telling you about the Lord and how He used to do things, He still does and He would love to answer your prayers. He loves you as much as He does this man and the woman injured by gunshot. He loves you enough to tell someone somewhere to pray for you. They are merely obeying God. God has His visiting angels all about us of which we are unaware. Remember what you have heard all your life. It is not scriptural, but it is literal: *"God works in mysterious ways."* And, so He does.

∽

INSTEAD OF GIVING UP—OVERCOME
by Shawn Scheffler

Here are 5 steps that I took to overcome, instead of giving up and quitting.

• **Dig Deep:** Look back to what was in you before LIFE seemed to define you. It is there, you just must peel back the layers. The deeper you dig into what is on the inside of you, the more you will realize what has been set aside or buried.

• **Dust off the dirt:** I know what you are thinking, that it's easier said than done and you are right! It is always easier to say something than it is to do it. However, when you have identified what you buried, it must be dusted off. I took the finished rough draft of my first book and sent it to editors I knew.

• **Don't Delay:** I started this blog post today. I was tired of gathering information, and decided to do what I like best, and that is to write. Whether it makes me any money today or not—I quit delaying. An you must get started also.

• **Deepen Your Faith:** For me, Faith in God is my key. *Hebrews 13:5* says, *"...For He Himself has said, I will never leave you nor forsake you."* This verse is an anchor to my soul; it is deep within me. No matter the outcome—God is faithful. *Faith* is defined as *the substance of things hoped for and the evidence of things not seen. (Hebrews 11:1)* Whether your faith is in God or not, FAITH is a spiritual principle anyone can put into practice. How can you deepen your faith? Start hoping for things you can't see. My family may not be together, but it hasn't stopped us from being one.

• **Do Something:** Today I set out to find a way to make more money. I looked at emails, followed links, and even revisited three mentors' websites. Then I visited my website and blog. I almost started to change the way my website and blog looked, and then, *"I quit—I quit trying to learn and started to write."*

The 5 things I just mentioned didn't just happen today. They are principles I have practiced anytime my mind feels like mush. They're things I do, when I need to do something.

FEAR NOT
by Paul Howard

I will not fear—
For You are with me.
I will not be dismayed,
On You, my foundation is laid.

You are my God,
I give you much praise,
You are my God,
My hands I raise.

I know that You will strengthen me,
Sometimes I need it so.
In times of trouble
To You I surely go.

I know that You will help me,
And helped, You always have.
You have always upheld me,
Upheld me with Your right hand.

Jesus is the answer.
When I'm in times of need,
He will always uphold me—
Fulfilling my every need.

~

A DECLARATION
OF GOD'S PROTECTION
by Charles Loghry

I WILL NOT FEAR – Father by your knowledge break up the depths of my despair and let Your glory clouds drop down the *heavenly dew,* let the dew saturate on my life, *(cf. Pr 3:20)* with Your grace, goodness, and mercy; so that, when I walk, I will walk safely and peacefully, that I will not stumble *(cf. Pr 3:23)* in the midst of darkness. When I lay down at night to rest my soul and body—I WILL NOT BE AFRAID, I will have sweet sleep, *(cf. Pr 3:24)* and in my dreams shall be the Voice of Your Holy Spirit guiding and ordering my every step. When I rise, I will not be afraid of sudden fear, neither will I be shaken by the desolation of the wicked when it comes; for the Lord is my confidence Who keeps my feet from being taken. *(See: Pr 3:25-26)*

He shall cause mine enemies that rise up against me, to be smitten before my face; enemies may come against me one way, but they shall flee from before me seven ways. *(cf. De 28:7)*

The Lord shall preserve me from all evil; He shall preserve my soul. The Lord shall preserve my going out and coming in, from this time forth, and even forever more. – Psalm 121:7-8

I know my God is on my side, I WILL NOT FEAR what man can do unto me. It is better for me to trust in the Lord, than to put confidence in man or princes. *(cf. Ps 118:8-9)* And I declare the Lord is my Helper—I WILL NOT FEAR what man shall do to me; *(cf. He 13:6)* for I am *a child of God. (cf. Ro 8:16)*

THE WEAPONS OF OUR WARFARE
are not of the flesh, but they are mighty through God to the destruction of human reasonings and strongholds of our enemies.
(2 Corinthians 10:4 pp.)

SALVATION

Mark 8:35
John 1:12, 29, 3:3, 16, 36
Acts 2:21, 3:19, 4:12, 10:43, 16:30-31
Romans 3:23-24, 5:6, 6:23, 10:9-10
2 Corinthians 5:17
Ephesians 2:8
Colossians 1:13-14, 20-22, 2:13-15
1 Peter 2:24
1 John 5:11

HEALING

Exodus 15:26
Psalms 103:3, 107:20
Proverbs 4:20-22, 17:22
Isaiah 53:5
Jeremiah 30:17
Malachi 4:2
Matthew 4:23, 8:7, 17
Mark 16:18
Luke 1:37, 9:6
John 14:14
Acts 5:16, 10:38

Romans 8:2
Galatians 3:13
Hebrews 2:14
James 5:14-16
1 Peter 2:24
3 John 2

AUTHORITY OVER SATAN

Isaiah 54:17
Matthew 7:29, 28:18, 10:7, 18:18
Luke 9:1, 10:19
John 12:31, 14:12, 30, 17:15
Romans 6:14, 8:37
1 Corinthians 15:57
2 Corinthians 10:4-5
Ephesians 1:3, 19-21, 4:27, 6:10-17
Colossians 2:10, 15
2 Timothy 1:7
Hebrews 10:13
1 Peter 5:8
1 John 4:4, 7
Revelations 12:11, 21:7

PROSPERITY

Genesis 2:11-12, 13:2, 24:35, 39:2-6
Deuteronomy 8:18, 16:17, 28:1-13
1 Kings 2:3
2 Chronicles 1:15
Psalm 1:1-3, 37:4, 105:37

Proverbs 3:9-10, 10:22, 13:22, 16:3, 21:20, 22:9, 28:27
Jeremiah 17:7-8
Malachi 3:8-10
Matthew 6:33
Luke 6:38, 16:10-11, 21:1-4
2 Corinthians 8:9, 9:6-8
Galatians 3:14, 3:29, 6:9
Philippians 4:19
3 John 2

PROTECTION

Deuteronomy 31:6
2 Samuel 22:3-4
Isaiah 41:10-14
Job 5:19-27
Psalm 5:11, 12:5, 20:1, 23:4, 34:19, 46:1, 57:1, 59:1, 91:1-16, 121:1-8, 138:7, 140:4
Proverbs 2:11
Isaiah 41:10-14, 54:17
Nahum 1:7
Matthew 6:13
Luke 1:68-75
Romans 8:31
2 Thessalonians 3:2-3
2 Timothy 4:18

CONTRIBUTING AUTHORS'
MINISTRY CONTACT INFORMATION
(In Alphabetical Order)

- **Adams, Paul Thomas**
Pastor Paul Thomas Adams
(918) 533-7721
oklahomamoses77@yahoo.com
Facebook: www.facebook.com/groups/200558138639060
9/'ELIYAHU MINISTRIES**ELIJAH'S WORD

- **Allday, Molly Sue**
Molly Allday Ministries
P.O. Box 701752
Tulsa, OK 74170
mollysmelodies@aol.com

- **Andrews, Jim and Sharon**
Glory In His Presence Ministry, Inc.
Tulsa, OK
(918) 663-5434
andrewszoe0@gmail.com

- **Blanchard, Len**
Pastor Len Blanchard
West Side Free Will Baptist Church
Sapulpa, OK
(918) 805-4926
www.westsidefwb.org
lbpreach@gmail.com

- **Bridges, Ginny**
Virginia Sue Barden Bridges
P.O. Box 3205
Pineville, LA 71361
ginrn1988@hotmail.com

- **Brophy, Renee**
Anointed Ones
c/oBrophy
7828 S Victor Ave., Apt. #6d
Tulsa, OK 74136
eagleatwar@hotmail.com

- **Burnes, Marcella O'Banion**
marcellaburnes@yahoo.com

- **Collins, Jan**
blessed2binhealth@gmail.com
<u>Facebook:</u> Jan - Young Living

- **Farmer, Steve**
Pastor Steve Farmer
Open Door Fellowship
405 East Taft
Sapulpa, OK 74066
www.OpenDoorFellowship.com

- **Gottlieb, Adrienne**
Adrienne Gottlieb, J.D.
Santa Fe, NM
www.GodsWisdomForWomen.com
agot@comcast.net
<u>Facebook:</u> God's Wisdom for Women

- **Harris, Mike**
Pastor Mike Harris
Beams of Light at Sapulpa
(918) 606-0469
www.beamsoflightatsapulpa.com
mikeeharris@cox.net

- **Hicks, Mike**
Minister Michael Hicks
P. O. Box 11491
Oklahoma City, OK 73136
www.YAHJireh.org and Facebook.
Mrhicks58@gmail.com
<u>*Facebook:*</u> Mike Hicks

- **Higgins, Bruce A.**
Bruce Higgins Ministries.
P. O. Box 691427
Tulsa, OK 74169
bahministries@att.net

- **Holloman, Daryl P**
P. O. Box 1649
Broken Arrow, OK 74013-1649 ▪ USA
dphwriter@yahoo.com

- **Howard, William Paul**
Claremore, OK
farmguy@hotmail.com

- **Marr, Ed**
Stone Bluff, Haskell, OK
(918) 574-5139
bigedvocal1@gmail.com

- **Martin, Collene**
Pearly White City Ministries
Crossville, TN 38571
(931) 510-7008
oswritemartin@gmail.com

- Neubauer, Marilyn
Dr. Marilyn Neubauer
www.marilynneubauer.com
P.O. Box 4664
Oceanside, CA 92052
(760) 439-1401

- **Nokes, Michael**
Michael Nokes Ministries
5103 S Sheridan Rd, #742
Tulsa, OK 74145
(918) 645-7517

- **Ohse, Brian**
Rev. Brian Ohse
Grace Ministries
(913) 416-3426
briandohse59@gmail.com

- **Sanders, Wayne**
Common Ground Ministries
P.O. Box 2811
Broken Arrow, OK 74013
(918) 455-4000
www.cgmok.com
waycom3@gmail.com

- **Scheffler, Shawn**
www.shawnscheffler.com
Facebook, instagram, LinkedIn: Shawn Scheffler
Twitter: @shawnscheffler

- **Steinmetz, William (Bill)**
Bill and Shirley Steinmetz
Casting Cares Ministries, Inc.
(918) 637-6412
Casting-Cares.org
Shirley@casting-cares.org

- **Stratton, Brandon**
Brandon Stratton River Ministries
Tulsa, OK
revstratton@gmail.com

- **Tattershall, Pam**
Rev. Pamela Tattershall
P.O. Box 141212
Broken Arrow, OK 74014
(918) 928-7304
anewdayministry.com
Pamela@anewdayministry.com

- **Tatum, Ruth**
Sapulpa, OK
Facebook: Ruth Tatum

- **Wear, Kim**
Kim Wear Ministries
629 Donegal Lane
Georgetown, Texas 78626
(816) 548-0990
kimkwear@yahoo.com

- **White, Barbara J.**
Faith Ministries International
P.O. Box 79126
Corona, CA 92879
fmint2010@hotmail.com
Facebook: Faith Ministries International
Facebook: Winning Widows

- **Wright, Landon Roy & Heather**
landonrwright@gmail.com

Check out these other Great Books from
BOLD TRUTH PUBLISHING

by Ed Marr
• FREEDOM *(3 Volume Series)*
An Comprehensive Biblical Study on True Repentance

-----

by Martha Johnson
• Our Story for His Glory
The Birth of a Church

------

by Dr. Marilyn Neubauer
• PRAYING for the Sick
— GUIDELINES —

-----

by Caleb Agadagba
• STRATEGIC PRAYER

-----

by Marcella O'Banion Burnes
• MENE, MENE, TEKEL UPHARSIN
Prophetic Poetry for these Perilous End-Times

See more Books and all of our products at
www.BoldTruthPublishing.com

▪ The song **"Come Into This Place"** Is on ITunes, Spotify and CD Baby! It is the first song on the CD *'Amazing Love' by Rachel Jeffries* The 2 CD album comes with <u>the words and background instrumental.</u> Order on *www.rjim.org*

Gain insight and boldness to step forward into an exciting life saving adventure of being led by the Spirit winning souls one-on-one in your everyday activities.

You will gain knowledge, experience and new found confidence as you learn to help people receive Jesus Christ into their hearts and be baptized in the precious Holy Spirit. Included in this Book: Instructions, Testimonies, Sample Scripts, an Outline for Evangelism, a Jump Start Plan and even a Gospel Tract for your use.

Available at select bookstores, Amazon and
www.BoldTruthPublishing.com

The hurt, lonely, oppressed and "called" are the heartbeat of prison ministry. The VICTORY is being able to reach out, touch another life and make a POSITIVE difference for the Glory of God!

Finally a practical teaching giving strategies for finding "hidden treasure" in Prison Ministry.

Available at select bookstores, Amazon and
www.BoldTruthPublishing.com

In this new devotional for women, Prophetic Evangelist and Teacher Kim Wear shares her heart and divine insights The Lord has whispered in her prayer times.

Whispers

A JOURNEY INTO HEARING GOD'S VOICE
by Kim Wear

"Whispers" is NOW ON KINDLE E-BOOK. Go to Amazon.com and put this wonderful inspired work on your Smart Phone or Tablet.

Available at select bookstores, Amazon and
www.BoldTruthPublishing.com

Five Smooth Stones

If you are facing a battle, this little book is
A MUST READ! You can defeat your Giants.
You can WIN over every attack.
The Word of God shows us how.

Made in the USA
Columbia, SC
12 May 2019